Chicago Streetcar Pictorial

The PCC Car Era
1936–1958

Jeffrey L. Wien
David Sadowski

Bradley Criss, Photo Editor

Bulletin 146 of the Central Electric Railfans' Association

Car 7213 laying over in the handsomely landscaped Clark-Arthur Loop opposite the Devon Station in August 1957.
Charles L. Tauscher, photo/Wien-Criss Archive

CERA Directors 2012		**CERA Directors 2013**	
John Anderson	Joseph Reuter	John A. Marton	William Reynolds
Tony Coppoletta	William Reynolds	John Nicholson	David Sadowski
Bradley Criss	Mark C. Walbrun	Joseph Reuter	Mark C. Walbrun
John A. Marton	Jeffrey L. Wien		Jeffrey L. Wien

CERA Bulletins are technical, educational references prepared as historic projects by members of the Central Electric Railfans' Association, working without salary due to their interest in the subject. This bulletin is consistent with this stated purpose of the corporation: To foster the study of the history, equipment, and operation of electric railways.

©2015 Central Electric Railfans' Association
An Illinois Not-for-Profit Corporation
P.O. Box 503, Chicago, Illinois, U.S.A.

Chicago Streetcar Memories
©2008 Chicago Transport Memories LLC

All rights reserved. No Part of this book may be commercially reproduced in any form, except for brief quotations, nor by any means electronic or mechanical, including photocopying and recording, nor by any informational storage retrieval system, without permission in writing from the Central Electric Railfans' Association.

Library of Congress Cataloging-in-Publication Data

Chicago streetcar pictorial : the PCC car era, 1936 to 1958 / edited by Jeffrey L. Wien, David Sadowski / Bradley Criss, Photo Editor.
  p. cm. – (Bulletin ... of Central Electric Railfans' Association ISSN 0069-1723 ; 146)
  Includes bibliographical references and index.
  ISBN 978-0-915348-46-6 (alk. paper)
  1. Street-railroads--Illinois--Chicago--History. I. Wien, Jeffrey L., editor of compilation. II. Central Electric Railfans' Assocation.

HE4491.C42C45 2015
625.409773'11--dc23

2015004088

Previous Page: Car 7049 heading northbound on State Street at Madison as a route 4 Cottage Grove car in June 1954. Carson Pirie Scott & Company was celebrating its one hundredth anniversary at the time.
Joseph Freed & Company Collection, used with permission

Table of Contents

Acknowledgements iv
Special Acknowledgement by David Sadowski v
About the Authors vi
Dedication vii

Forward 1
Chicago's Streetcar Corporate History Synopsis 3
The Rise and Fall of the Modern Streetcar in Chicago 5
Map of Streetcar Lines (as of 1950) 38

4 Cottage Grove 54
8 Halsted 98
20 Madison - Madison/Fifth 114
22 Clark-Wentworth 134
36 Broadway-State 236
    Andre Kristopans' Story 282
42 Halsted/Downtown 302
49 Western 306
63 63rd Street 364

The Last Chicago Streetcar 391
Preserved Chicago PCC Cars 395
    4021 story 395
    4391 Story 397
    The Story of the Acquisition of CTA PCC 4391 by Frank Hicks 399
Tribute PCCs in Kenosha and San Francisco 423

PCC Roster 428
Chicago PCC Trivia 429
1936 PCCs Car Plan 430
St. Louis Car Company Post-War PCCs Car Plan 431
Pullman-Standard Post-War PCCs Car Plan 432
One-man Conversion PCCs Car Plan 433

Putting it Together by Bradley Criss, Photo Editor 435
Bibliography 438
DVD: Chicago Streetcar Memories .... 440, Back Cover

Acknowledgments

It took many dedicated individuals working for both the Chicago Surface Lines and the Chicago Transit Authority to keep the city's "Blue Geese" and "Green Hornets" operating on time and in all conditions over the streets of Chicago. Motormen, conductors, shop men, supervisors, and managers all worked together to ensure that Chicago's streetcar service was second to none.

Likewise it takes the work of many dedicated historians and photographers to preserve and chronicle the events and images of Chicago's transit past. We are indeed fortunate that so many traction enthusiasts were out photographing the Second City's streetcars in all locales, whether it was in summer's brilliant sunlight or on those cold, drab winter days that are familiar to all Chicagoans.

We would like to thank the following photographers whose work and contributions made this book possible: Eric Bronsky; James J. Buckley; R. Burns; Frank E. Butts; Richard C. Cerne; Raymond DeGroote; Thomas H. Desnoyers; George H. Forman; Robert W. Gibson; Truman D. Hefner; Robert D. Heinlein; Frank Hicks; William C. Hoffman; William C. Janssen; Ronald J. Johnson; John E. Koschwanez; Larry Kostka; George Krambles; Gordon E. Lloyd; John Marton; Robert V. Mehlenbeck; Frank J. Misek; Bernhardt L. Neuberger; Greer Nielsen; John Pilling, Jr.; Bernard A. Rossbach; David Sadowski; Kenneth J. Spengler; Henry Stange, Jr.; Bernard L. Stone; Charles L. Tauscher; Charles H. Thorpe; Eugene Van Dusen; Jeffrey L. Wien; and John R. Williams.

We were fortunate to be granted access to the Krambles-Peterson Archive through the cooperation of Art Peterson and we also wish to express our gratitude to George Kanary for sharing images from the Electric Railway Historical Society Collection. We are also grateful to those providing photos from the John Bromley Collection, the Richard Krisak Collection, the Michael Raia Collection, the Joseph Freed & Company Collection, the CTA Historical Collection, and the CERA Archives.

Special thanks go out to Bernard Rossbach who provided us with rare original copies of 1936 Chicago newspapers featuring stories and advertisements covering the debut of Chicago's first PCC cars. We would also like to thank Dennis McClendon for his excellent system map. We are grateful to Andre Kristopans for additional details on the tragic accident of May 25, 1950.

We would also like to thank John Nicholson for his involvement in the early stages of preparing the text, selecting photos and his final proofing of the book.

Most of all we would like to thank Bradley Criss for his work in the design and layout of this book as well as his work on retouching and color correcting the photographs that appear. We appreciate not only his talent, but his patience with the editors in times of deadline-related stress.

It was a team effort—the fusion of many styles and personalities that brought about this book which we hope will bring back many fond memories for older readers and inspire younger ones to discover more about Chicago's transportation past.

Jeff Wien and David Sadowski

Special Acknowledgment

There was a fateful moment in June 1956, when the teenaged Jeff Wien discovered that the CTA Route 49 Western Avenue streetcar line had been converted to bus. It was then he realized that Chicago's streetcars were fast disappearing, and would soon be ignominiously consigned to the "dustbin of history." The average person took little notice.

PCC 4401 at Clark/Howard Terminal on September 7, 1957. This was the last Clark Streetcar with Motorman Matt Butler and Conductor James Brown. Jeffrey L. Wien is taking a photo. (CTA Historical Photograph Collection)

Emboldened, he began to document the shrinking streetcar system in every way he possibly could. Sometimes, when passersby would spot him standing on the curb filming PCCs with his 8mm movie camera, they were incredulous. "Why," they would ask, "would anyone want to take a picture of a streetcar?" Soon enough, Jeff discovered there were a few other people who felt the same way he did. And from that day forward, Jeff Wien has been there every step of the way, in his mission to preserve the history of Chicago's once mighty streetcar network for future generations.

When the last Chicago PCC ran the rails in the early hours of June 21, 1958, Jeff was on that car, having helped drape it with crepe paper. When car 4391 was trucked to a farm in Downers Grove, Jeff was there. When the lone surviving postwar PCC made its way to the Illinois Railway Museum, where it began running again in 1975, Jeff was there. And when the Chicago Transit Authority had car 4391 brought back to Daley Plaza, to celebrate CTA's 40th anniversary, Jeff was there to see things come full circle.

From the late 1950s on, when he risked being arrested while roaming the junkyards of Chicago, in his quest to document the final days of our discarded streetcars, Jeff has been steadfast and determined. I am reminded of the late Richard Nickel, crawling around in the ruins of Louis Sullivan masterpieces as they fell to the wrecking ball. In the short term, the wrecking ball carried the day, but in time, history has proven both Richard Nickel and Jeff Wien right.

Within the pages of this book, you will find a veritable "Lost Chicago." Along with pictures of PCC streetcars, you will also see long-gone neighborhoods, men with brimmed hats, women in their flowing summer dresses, movie palaces and other architectural gems, and a wealth of 1950s automobiles, with their two-tone paint jobs and huge fins- in other words, a portrait of a vanished way of life. A "love letter" to a Chicago that once was.

Jeffrey Wien has been a friend and mentor to me and many other railfans for a long time. Without Jeff's vision, doggedness, and determination, the book you hold in your hands today, and much of the history in it, would not exist today and could hardly be possible. He has collected a wealth of material that no one else has. This book was his idea, and it is largely due to his enthusiasm and perfectionism that we have seen it through to completion. He has practically a photographic memory for locations, and has often been able to identify where pictures were taken by noticing the minutest of details that would escape anyone else.

If I have been able to help Jeff realize his vision for this book, even in a small way, I am gratified. It is his life's work and his true legacy. I thank him for it, and you, the reader, should thank him for it as well. Thank you, Jeff, for a job well done.

David Sadowski, March 2014

About the Authors

Jeffrey L. Wien

Long before he rode Chicago's very last streetcar in 1958, Jeff Wien had been an avid traction enthusiast. Sensing that the days of Chicago's streetcars were numbered, he began photographing the remaining lines in 1956 while still in his teens. Jeff also enjoyed a short but memorable period as an employee of the North Shore Line and was on board for the last southbound trip in 1963. Still a very active transit photographer, Jeff has also been involved in equipment preservation through his work at the Illinois Railway Museum. A longtime CERA member as well, Jeff has contributed much of his time and talent to CERA publications and activities.

David Sadowski

Ever since his first ride on a Chicago streetcar at age three, Dave Sadowski has remained close to the sights and sounds of electric traction. A visit to view the stored Chicago Aurora and Elgin cars at Wheaton in the early 60s piqued his interest in interurbans and a trip on the Skokie Swift as one the very first riders cemented it. Over the years Dave has had the opportunity to visit and photograph many transit properties across the country and has made an in-depth study of the operations and finances of many of these companies. A member of CERA since 1983, Dave has served on the Board of Directors and undertaken many tasks for the organization over the years.

Dedication

To the trainmen, employees, and managers of the Chicago Surface Lines on their centenary, February 1, 1914.

And to all the railfans who photographed the Chicago streetcar system creating a rich collection of photography for us to draw upon for this book.

Foreword

Ask anyone who has ever ridden a modern Chicago streetcar what it was like, and they will tell you that is was unlike any other type of vehicle that one could ride in a city street. The cars seemed to quietly glide down the street without the bumpy sensations found on a modern motor bus, trolley bus, or automobile. With their trucks hidden behind full skirts, they looked as though they were floating on air.

In the late 1930s, the Chicago Surface Lines brought the concept of the modern streetcar to the city when 83 new PCC cars began operation on Madison Street. These new streetcars were called PCC cars because they had been conceived by a group of electric street railway executives called the Presidents' Conference Committee (PCC). After the end of the Second World War, the Chicago Surface Lines purchased 600 more PCC cars with the thought that this large fleet of modern streetcars would serve the citizens of the city for decades to come; yet these same cars disappeared from Chicago's streets in little more than a decade.

Through photographs, we will take you on a journey covering the eight streetcar lines that were equipped with PCC cars by the Chicago Surface Lines and later the Chicago Transit Authority between 1936 and 1958. This book will be many things to many people. The traction enthusiast or urban transit student will discover a variety of routes and locales—North Side, South Side, and West Side—as cars negotiated their way over crowded streets or skimmed along on private rights-of-way. Older readers will remember riding the PCC cars through neighborhoods bustling with activity—the "Mom-and-Pop" stores, all those brands of Chicago-brewed beer, those black finial-capped traffic lights on almost every corner, and the neighborhood taverns that seemed to outnumber the traffic lights. These scenes, like prominent landmarks of the era (the Red Star Inn, the Morrison Hotel, and the Sherman House, among others) have vanished forever from our cityscape along with the streetcars that ran by their doors.

For younger readers, this book will open a door to the past, to a different—and to us—a much more fascinating way of life. We hope that through these pages they will gain an appreciation of why Chicago's streetcars (in this case the PCC cars) hold a special place in the hearts of many Chicagoans and why they are still so fondly remembered almost six decades after their demise.

We will cover the eight lines that operated PCCs from their northern terminals to their southern terminals and from their western terminals to their eastern terminals. So, pay your fare to the conductor at the rear of the car and take a seat. You won't have time to read your *Daily News* or *American* as you will be too busy looking out the window and observing a world of motion and color (such as Mercury Green, Croydon Cream, and Swamp Holly Orange).

Welcome Aboard!

Previous Page: Car 4361 at State and Jackson in December 1953.
James J. Buckley, photo/CERA Archives

Southbound PCC 4060 passes the entrance to Riverview Amusement Park at Western and Roscoe in June 1956. Riders were urged by television personality "Two-Ton" Baker to visit the park and "laugh their troubles away."
William C. Hoffman, photo/Wien-Criss Archive

Chicago's Streetcar Corporate History Synopsis

Horse drawn streetcars first began plying the streets of Chicago in 1859. They were operated by the North Chicago City Railway Company on the North Side; on the South Side they were under the control of the Chicago City Railway Company.

Between 1859 and 1914, the North and West sides of the city developed a network of streetcar lines through a series of mergers and acquisitions which ultimately resulted in the creation of the Chicago Railways Company. The South and Southeast Side streetcar networks were developed by three major companies and their predecessors: the Chicago City Railway Company, the Southern Street Railway Company, and the Calumet and South Chicago Railway Company. In 1908, the properties of the Calumet and South Chicago Railway Company were acquired under an operating agreement by the Chicago City Railway Company. The following year (1909), the Chicago City Railway acquired the properties of the Southern Street Railway under a similar operating agreement. Thus, by 1909, the Chicago City Railway Company controlled the streetcar operations from the Loop south and east to the Chicago city limits.

For a number of years at the end of the nineteenth and the beginning of the twentieth century, city politicians clamored for the consolidation of the various streetcar companies into one operation. Finally after much political wrangling, the Chicago City Council adopted the Traction Unification Ordinance on November 13, 1913, which took effect on February 1, 1914. At that time the properties of the Chicago Railways Company, Chicago City Railway Company, Calumet and South Chicago Railway, and the Southern Street Railway Company were consolidated under a new name: Chicago Surface Lines.

The operations of the Chicago Surface Lines continued through September 30, 1947. On October 1, 1947, the properties of the Chicago Surface Lines were acquired by the Chicago Transit Authority (CTA). The CTA also acquired the properties of the Chicago Rapid Transit Company at the same time. CTA's acquisition of the Surface Lines and the Rapid Transit operations brought Chicago's transit services under a truly unified management with the exception of the Chicago Motor Coach Company, which was acquired on October 1, 1952.

CSL Banner at Municipal (Navy) Pier in 1921.
Chicago Transit Authority Collection

Chicago Surface Lines artist's conception of Car 4001 built by Pullman-Standard in 1934 which was a pre-PCC car.
CERA Archives

The Rise and Fall of the Modern Streetcar in Chicago

As the "Roaring Twenties" came to a close in 1929, just before the onset of the Great Depression, the concern of many large streetcar operators in American cities was the fact that their ridership was on a steady decline. The principal cause of the decline was the rapid rise in popularity of the automobile. Henry Ford, General Motors, Chrysler and a multiplicity of automobile manufacturers had placed the automobile within economic reach of the ordinary worker. One did not have to possess extreme wealth to afford an automobile. As more autos crowded the streets of the cities, streetcar operators found it increasingly difficult to maintain schedules. The streetcar fleets consisted of equipment that was slow, noisy, had uncomfortable seating, indifferent heat, and poor ventilation. The operators of those streetcar systems realized that if they were going to preserve their investments in their streetcar networks, they had to do something to bring riders back to their car lines. The only way to do that was to develop a modern streetcar that would be as fast as the autos against which it competed. To succeed, this modern streetcar would also have to provide a smooth quiet ride, offer comfortable seating, and proper ventilation.

To this end, the American Electric Railway Association (AERA), a trade organization consisting of the major streetcar operators in the United States, created an advisory committee in the fall of 1929, which it called the Electric Railway Presidents' Conference Committee (ERPCC). With the passage of time the ERPCC became known more simply as the Presidents' Conference Committee (PCC). The committee consisted of leaders of both operating companies and the transit manufacturing industry. It was given the assignment of conducting a three-year research program to develop the principles that would be embodied in the design of a new streetcar suited to modern conditions.

One of the members of the PCC was Guy A. Richardson, who had become president of the Chicago Surface Lines (CSL) in 1932. The CSL at the time was the largest street railway operator in the world under one management with a fleet of 3,268 passenger cars, 11,550 trainmen, and 1,059 miles of track. On August 5, 1921, CSL proudly proclaimed these statistics on promotional banners it had set up at Chicago's Municipal (later Navy) Pier streetcar terminal.

Guy Richardson was a strong proponent of the modern streetcar and was eager to have a fleet of modern cars running in Chicago. To that end the Surface Lines obtained two experimental streetcars in 1934 which were designed along the principles set forth by the Presidents' Conference Committee.

Car 4001 at 78th and Vincennes in July 1936.
John Bromley Collection

Chicago Surface Lines artist's conception of Car 7001 built by the J.G. Brill Company in 1934 which was a pre-PCC car.
CERA Archives

1935 production model of pre-PCC car built by the St. Louis Car Company in Washington, DC; operated by Capital Transit Company.
Charles L. Tauscher Photo/Wien-Criss Archive

Car 7001 at State and Chicago in the summer of 1934.
Krisak-Bushnell Photo Archive

Car 4001 at Vincennes and 78th in May 1937.
CERA Archives

After two years of operating experience, it was possible to write specifications for the new streetcars which were radically different from any equipment that was operated at the time. These specifications were adopted by the Presidents' Conference Committee and were embodied into what became known as the PCC (Presidents' Conference Committee) car.

1936 PCCs

On February 28, 1936, the Board of Operations of the Chicago Surface Lines placed an order for 83 PCC cars with the St. Louis Car Company at a cost of $15,296 per car; these were purchased with the intent of fully equipping the Madison Street car line. The new cars were two-man, operated by a motorman and a conductor, and were front entrance cars similar to motor and trolley buses. The new PCC cars encompassed the latest in technological innovations such as steel wheels with rubber inserts to reduce noise level, forced air ventilation, leather-bound seats, and powerful electric motors which permitted rapid rates of acceleration. They were 50 feet 5 inches long and 8 feet 8 inches wide. As such they were the longest single-end streetcars ever built in the United States. Most American cities purchased PCC cars that were 46 feet long and 8 feet four inches wide. This compares to a standard motor bus which is 40 feet in length or an articulated motor bus that is 60 feet in length.

By 1936, many large cities were beginning to consider the motor bus and trolley bus viable alternatives to new streetcars such as the PCC car. So it was in September 1936 that Surface Lines President Guy Richardson made the following address to the American Transit Association convention regarding the advantage of the modern streetcar in large cities:

> The assignment of the subject "Continuing Need for the Street Car in Urban Transit," which I am asked to discuss briefly, indicates on the part of some a faltering faith, if not actual disbelief, in the street car as a useful tool of the transportation industry of the future. Otherwise, there would be no point in discussing the subject before this convention. The street car needs no defense. It is and will continue to be indispensable in urban transportation in the larger cities.
>
> This is not my opinion alone. The leaders of this industry came to that conclusion some six years ago when the Presidents' Conference Committee was organized for the purpose of improving and modernizing street railway equipment. They recognized the continuing need of the street car in urban transportation and set about building a car that would completely fill that need.
>
> The committee has accomplished its purpose. With the co-operation of electric railway managements and equipment manufacturers, it has given us a new street car that should

Surface Service Magazine

A Monthly Publication by and for Chicago Surface Lines Employes

VOL. 13   NOVEMBER, 1936   No. 8

New Cars Arrive

Sensation Created by First of Streamlined Equipment

The new cars are here—that is, the first of them are.

The reception given them upon their introduction to the people of Chicago on Thursday and Friday, November 12 and 13, demonstrated the fact that this new type of equipment is really a sensation in the local transportation world.

The first introduction was at a huge parade along West Madison street organized and conducted under the auspices of the West Side Traffic and Transportation Association, an organization comprising all of the west side civic and improvement groups. The new cars were preceded by floats showing older type horse-drawn equipment and an early type of electric car used in Chicago soon after the electrification of the lines. In the new cars were public officials and officers of civic and improvement organizations. Preceding and following this Surface Lines pageant of transportation were numerous floats provided by west side business men.

On Friday the new cars were exhibited to the public at State and Adams street, and thousands of interested people filed through them, inspecting the many innovations in street car construction.

First Car Arrives

The first of the new cars, No. 7002, arrived in Chicago on a flat car on Saturday, October 24. It was delivered at the South Shops and was immediately turned over to the mechanical force which proceeded to check it over and see that it was in good operating condition.

The following Saturday the second car arrived and since then four others have been received.

Selected men from both the mechanical and train force have been familiarizing themselves with the new equipment and already a considerable number of men are trained to handle these and other cars as they are received.

Completing Two a Day

At the St. Louis Car Company, Chicago Surface Lines cars are going along the assembly line and will be turned out at the rate of two a day until the entire order of 83 cars has been filled. It is anticipated that early in December it will be possible to equip fully the Madison street line with the new cars.

From the public standpoint, the most noticeable feature of the new equipment is its quietness. The cars glide down the street so silently that pedestrians stop and stare at them and wonder what has happened to the noises a street car is supposed to make.

Those who have ridden on the cars, however, exclaim at the smoothness of their operation, the comfort of the seats, the bright illumination without glare, and the abundance of clean fresh air provided by the ventilating system.

It is generally agreed that this is the most sensational development in local transportation in a generation.

Wide-Spread Publicity

The newspapers of the city have devoted columns of space to description and illustration of the new cars. The Chicago *Tribune* published on the morning of November 12 an 8-page section devoted exclusively to this new equipment. All of the community papers have given considerable space to descriptive matter. The State Street Council co-operated in calling attention to the new cars by placing window cards in their show windows and distributing a folder prepared by the Surface Lines for the occasion. West Madison street was decorated by the merchants from the west city limits to Canal street.

From all parts of the city requests have been received from civic and improvement groups asking that the new cars be exhibited in their localities.

Description of the Cars

The following is a brief description of the new cars:

They are of the front-entrance, center and rear exit type, equipped with "blinker" doors.

The cars are 50 feet 5 inches long, 8 feet 9 inches wide, and 10 feet high from rail to the top of the roof. They have a seating capacity of 58 passengers. They weigh only 35,000 pounds, which is about 10,000 pounds less than the last cars purchased by the Chicago Surface Lines a few years ago.

Specially designed seats providing ample knee room are used in the cars. The backs of the seats are padded, sloped and shaped so as to afford the greatest degree of comfort.

Adequate stanchions and hand-holds on the backs of the seats are an important aid to moving or standing passengers.

The interior of the car is attractively finished with stainless steel trim.

The material used in the floor will not become slippery in wet weather.

surpass in performance, in economy of operation and in public appeal, any transportation vehicle that the automotive industry has been able to produce.

Years of effort and hundreds of thousands of dollars were spent in producing a car to meet the requirements of modern street and traffic conditions. A large number of these cars have been ordered from the manufacturers and they will soon be on the streets of several cities, demonstrating what they can do.

After this demonstration is made the question as to the continuing need of the street car in urban transit will no longer be asked. The new cars themselves will answer the question. No longer will we be comparing 1915 street cars with 1936 buses. The bus will have to show its value in rider appeal, in economy of operation, and in efficient use of street space, in comparison with a vehicle which can operate at lower costs and with increased efficiency where large numbers of passengers are to be carried.

In the new vehicle the rattle and bang of the old street car has been eliminated. It glides along its smooth steel rail surface and even over crossings and switches as quietly as the passing automobile and much more quietly than buses or trucks. The smoothness and comfort of the ride it provides are certain to be preferred by the passengers to the swerving and jolting bus as it rolls over the uneven pavement of the streets. Its electric heating, lighting and ventilation are superior to anything that can be provided in a gasoline bus. The new car will hold its place in street traffic because of its speed of acceleration and braking efficiency.

Street cars have some very definite advantages in urban transportation:

First   On busier streets service by street car is faster, more comfortable, safer, less expensive, and causes less interference to other street users than the equivalent service by any other carrier.

Second   Electric heating, lighting, and ventilating add to the comfort of passengers.

Third   Drawing its power from a central power station and operating with electric motors, the street car has fewer failures in traffic and operates at much less energy cost.

Fourth   This lower power cost and the larger number of passengers that can be carried per unit make possible economies which result in lower rates of fare or improved service.

Fifth   The street car, operating on a fixed track, does not straddle traffic lanes and causes less street congestion, thus serving public convenience by utilizing street space to the best advantage.

Finally, it must be admitted that it is worthwhile to prevent the destruction of billions of dollars of invested capital by the junking of street railways and the substitution of a service which cannot be as economic or as satisfactory in large centers of population.

I scarcely need to say that it is not my intention to give you the impression that I am against buses and trolley buses. In the short space of time allotted to me I have merely tried to keep to the main subject that there is a continuing need for street cars in urban transit.

All surface transportation systems in the country now are making use of buses and a great many of them are using trolley buses. There is a wide field for both and undoubtedly there are smaller cities where it is advisable to abandon street car lines and substitute buses because buses will better serve the particular type of territory involved. In any large city surface transportation where various traffic density conditions exist, there is need for street cars, trolley buses, and automotive buses of various sizes.

The properly balanced surface system- I am not discussing rapid transit, for that is a subject in itself- I repeat, the properly balanced surface system will use all of these facilities.

I am convinced, however, that when all of the shouting and tumult over the automotive vehicle has quieted down so that we can see more clearly the needs of urban transit, more and more use will be made of electrically propelled vehicles.

Experimental Car on Milwaukee

Engineers Study Reactions of Riding Public to New Vehicle

For the last four weeks an unusual car has been in service on the Milwaukee avenue line—unusual in that it is a vehicle differing in appearance and operation from the regular type of car used on that line. The car is different. In some respects it is unlike any other operated by the Chicago Surface Lines.

The car, No. 4051, is being operated for experimental purposes. It is a fast, streamlined vehicle, resembling in appearance the PCC cars operating on the Madison street line. It is, in fact, one of the Madison street cars which has been reconstructed to make an important change in type of operation. Instead of a front entrance car, like the other Madison street vehicles, it is a rear entrance car.

The change, for test purposes, was authorized by the Surface Lines Car Design Committee. This committee, after many months of discussion of the relative merits of front and rear loading, authorized the rebuilding of this car, to make possible a comparison of the two principles of passenger handling in modern vehicles. Practically all of the street cars built in the country in recent years have been the front entrance style and there have been no comprehensive tests made of the rear entrance principle on modern cars.

Substantially Rebuilt

The change from front to rear entrance required substantial rebuilding of the interior of the car as well as the right side of the exterior. The work was done at the West Shops. Like the Madison street cars, car 4051 is a "single-end" unit; that is, one which has the motorman's controls at only one end of the car. Milwaukee avenue was selected for the test because it is a heavily traveled line where all the cars regularly operated are of the rear entrance type. This assured that passengers would be following their usual habit of boarding at the rear.

An exterior view of car No. 4051 shows the three rear doors which are used for loading on this experimental car.

Car No. 4051 has three doors at the rear, one at the center and two at the front. Passengers enter at the rear and can select any of three locations for leaving—two doors at the front, one at the center and one at the rear. The rear exit door also serves as one of three loading doors. On the regular Madison street cars, passengers board at three entrance doors at the front and leave through two center and one rear exit doors. The motorman's position on car 4051 is unchanged, but the conductor, instead of being at the center exit doors, is stationed at the rear on the left side of the car.

Seek Further Improvement

The purpose of the experiment with this type of car, it is explained, is to find if further improvements in passenger convenience and comfort can be made. The front entrance PCC car, which was introduced four years ago, represented the most forward step taken by the industry in many, many years. But efforts are constantly being made to devise improvements even on this advanced type of vehicle, so that when orders for new units may be placed, the latest models will be better than the preceding ones.

It is emphasized by members of the Car Design Committee that the experiment with the rear entrance feature does not necessarily mean that new cars built in the future will be of this design. The committee, however, does wish to have the benefit of all possible research and experiment when preparing specifications for new cars to serve trunk lines.

The performance of the car and the reactions of passengers to its innovations are being studied closely by Surface Lines engineers. From this study, the Car Design Committee expects to determine, after weighing the relative advantages of front and rear entrance models, which type is better suited to various kinds of service.

This interior view shows how the conductor is stationed in the rear. Front and center doors are recommended to alighting passengers.

> The reason for this is obvious. The cost of gasoline and oil is tending constantly to increase because of the tendency of government to add taxes to their price and because, also, of the progressive depletion of available crude oil supplies. On the other hand, the cost of electricity has shown a downward trend over the past several years, and the indications are that as electricity use increases, the price curve will continue to go lower.
>
> From the economic standpoint alone, therefore, it seems to me that urban transportation operators will be compelled to rely more upon electrically propelled vehicles and to restrict the use of automotive vehicles to routes where the volume of riding does not warrant the larger capital expenditures required for electrical propulsion.
>
> If the new street car lives up to expectations, not only should most of the present investment in rail lines prove a valuable asset, but new rail lines will be laid as extensions of existing lines and in territory now served by gasoline or trolley buses as it builds up to a point where a heavier investment is warranted.
>
> In other words, I go a step further than the subject assigned to me. I not only believe there is a continuing need for street cars in urban transit, but I am convinced that in large cities they will have an increasing value.

On November 12, 1936, CSL placed the first six of the 83 PCC cars in service on Madison Street. Huge crowds lined the route that evening to welcome the new cars to the city as reported in CSL's *Surface Service* of November 1936 reproduced on the facing page.

After the dedication of the new PCC streetcars, it was reported that the Surface Lines management was so pleased with their performance that CSL President Richardson made it known that he hoped that the Surface Lines would be able to have a fleet of 1,035 PCC cars in the foreseeable future.

At the time that the new PCC cars, nicknamed "Streamliners" by the CSL, entered service, it was stated that the operation of streetcars on Madison Street would in effect be an operational laboratory

Car 4005 on Madison in Garfield Park on November 24, 1936.
Westinghouse Photo/John Bromley Collection

Facing Page: "Experimental Car on Milwaukee Avenue," *Surface Service*, Otober 1940.
Wien-Criss Archive

Model of Car 4020 which was outshopped in October 1945 in the Marigold Yellow color.
John Bromley Collection

Model of Car 4022 which was outshopped in November 1945 in the Clipper Blue color.
John Bromley Collection

Model of Car 4050 which was outshopped in December 1945 in the Coronado Tan color.
John Bromley Collection

Model of Car 4035 which was outshopped in November 1945 in the orange color with a maroon V-front.
John Bromley Collection

Model of Car 4010 which was outshopped in October 1945 in the Venetian Red color.
John Bromley Collection

Model of Car 4018 which was outshopped in November 1945 in a variation of the Mercury Green, Croydon Cream, and Swamp Holly Orange colors that were adopted for the postwar PCC cars.
John Bromley Collection

in which the cars would be evaluated to provide background for further renewal of equipment. It should be noted that although the Surface Lines referred to the new cars as "Streamliners," trolley enthusiasts alternately assigned the monikers of "Blue Geese" or "Blue Devils" to them, probably due to their dark blue and cream colors with a red belt rail.

Then in 1940, the Surface Lines conducted another experiment using PCC car number 4051. As stated in the October 1940 issue of *Surface Service*, the door configuration of the car was changed so that it was converted into a rear entrance car. It was operated on Milwaukee Avenue, a route that used rear entrance cars, to see how effective a rear entrance PCC car would be.

Management felt there were too many possibilities to avoid fare payment with the pay-as-you-pass system then in use on the 1936 cars.

Riders of the car were interviewed during the test period to get their opinion about the new streetcar. As things later turned out the rear entrance configuration would become the door arrangement that the Surface Lines adopted when it placed its next order for new PCC cars.

With Guy Richardson's dream of over 1,000 PCC streetcars in mind, the Surface Lines was ready to begin ordering new cars in 1941; however, world events intervened. By 1940, with Europe enveloped in a major war between Great Britain and France on one side and Germany on the other, the United States realized it had better start preparing itself militarily in the event it too was drawn into the European conflict as it had been in the previous war. A national draft was inaugurated in 1940 and defense spending was increased significantly. While the European conflict drew the most attention, Japan was engaging in territorial aggression in its war against China which had begun in 1937. On June 22, 1941, Germany attacked the Soviet Union resulting in an all-out war over the European continent. Any desire on the part of the Surface Lines to order more PCC cars was put on "hold" as the nation braced itself for war. Then came the Japanese attack on Pearl Harbor on December 7, 1941, which resulted in war being declared on Japan; four days later Germany and Italy declared war on the United States. From that point onward, the US found itself fighting both European and Pacific wars in what became known as the Second World War.

During the war, the Surface Lines did the best it could to keep its fleet of 3,600 older cars running "for the duration." In 1945, CSL altered the color scheme of its Madison Street streamliners by adding striping to the fronts of the cars as related in a *Surface Service* article from October-November 1945 reproduced on the next page.

Also during 1945, CSL conducted a test using six of the Madison Street cars, painting each in a different color scheme to see which livery the public most preferred. The colors finally adopted for the postwar cars were Mercury Green, Croydon Cream, and Swamp Holly Orange.

Color movies of the pre-war PCC cars in the various experimental color schemes can be found in the attached *Chicago Streetcar Memories* DVD in Chapter 10, which is titled "Postwar PCCs."

Model of postwar PCC car in Mercury Green, Croydon Cream and Swamp Holly Orange colors.
Eric Bronsky Photo/George Kanary Layout

Seventy-seventh Street — Dorothy Musial

WE EXPRESS our deep sympathy to the families of the late *T. O'Donnell*, conductor, *H. Schuelke*, supervisor, and *Ass't. Superintendent J. Becker*, whose father passed away last month . . . Welcome home, *C. Carey*, but don't spring any of the French stuff on us . . . It has been suggested to us that we adopt the hobby of collecting all those multi-colored shirts that our trainmen have been wearing during the war. Not a bad idea at that! *J. Blais*, conductor, can very well supply us with some gaudy ties to complete the ensemble . . . A year ago this month, your scribe had a write-up about a pencil *Melvin Clausen* possessed. We claimed it to be the envy of every conductor, because of its large size. In reply to the write-up, we received an invitation to visit the Hobby Show, from *Ted Shuman*, scribe at Armitage, who had a booth there. To our chagrin we found that in his booth, Ted has not only the largest pencil in the world, but also the smallest, and every size, shape and style of pencil in captivity. Due to the fact that Ted outshines us in the line of pencils, I won't even mention the fact that *Mr. Duncan*, chief clerk, has a three-foot pencil in his possession . . . The following trainmen have taken their pensions effective October 1: *A. L. Hildebrand, T. Morris, M. L. Baker*, and *R. P. Wilson (No. 1)*. Congratulations and the best of luck to four of our best trainmen . . . I'm sure we all remember the fine work *Mike Tierney* did in inducting men into the Marines during the War. Well the rewards are coming in for his wonderful work. *Joseph McCarthy*, a fireman, who was one of Mike's "Boys" (as he calls them) received the Congressional Medal of Honor from President Truman . . . The Golden Wedding of *Philias Bessette*, a retired barn man of Archer, Sunday, Sept. 16, 1945, is a day long to be remembered. *Superintendent W. A. Bessette* of 77th, a brother of the groom, and his wife, marched down the church aisle in the wedding party.

Accident Investigation — Audrey Johnson

SYMPATHY of the department is expressed to *Stenographer Jerry Burak* and *Typist Margaret O'Donnell*, whose fathers passed away recently . . . Sympathy of the department is also expressed to Accident Investigator Samuel Fisher whose brother passed away.

John O'Neill, Yeoman 1st Class, just in from Manila via Seattle on a ten day leave, dropped in to say hello . . . *Colonel Leigh H. Hunt* surprised us with a visit after a 10,000 mile hop from the South Pacific. John went back to Seattle and Col. Leigh expected to leave for Washington, D. C. Hope both you fellows will be back for good soon.

A hearty welcome is extended to *Clerks Edna Bruzzino* and *Lucille Burke*, *Stenographer Anna Krautsak* and *Locator Earl F. Foster*. They say it's better late than never, so here's letting *Stenographer Reggie Kuzius* know that it's nice having her back with us again.

Howard (Alabam) Doster, former messenger boy, found his way up here from Dothan. He was here to see the All Stars. We almost needed an interpreter, but we did enjoy hearing, in that deep southern drawl, about his experiences both in the Army and subsequent civilian life.

Attorney Fred W. Kinderman is a proud daddy for the second time. Thanks for the candy and cigars you passed around in honor of the young lady, Janet, born September 21, 1945.

First Lt. Bill Connolly, Jr., is the first of our servicemen to be back working with us at "600." Bill was with the 99th Infantry Division and saw a lot of action in Europe.

Sympathy of the Department is expressed to *Statementman John J. Davis* whose father passed away.

We can't decide which outsparkled the other, *Shirley Lull's* eyes or the diamond she wore. Here's wishing you happiness. Hope that *Private Thomas McCabe* will be back home soon.

MAE WEST, IN REVERSE—Making like ladies, the pin-up cars of West Madison have gotten themselves a new face-do—but with the un-ladylike goal of appearing broader in the beam. . . . Seems that oncoming traffic tended to snuggle up to the old paint job; failed to give it a wide-enough berth. . . . The new paint job, emphasizing all the right places, fairly shouts, "Gimme the run-around; I'm a dangerous dame!"

Accounting — By Thomas F. Coan

THE ACCOUNTING DEPARTMENT'S heartiest congratulations and best wishes are extended to *Mr. Erven Guy* for success in his new office appointment as Assistant Auditor.

Birthday greetings were extended to *Rosemary Eme, Natalie Kaczkowski, Helen Gerke, Elizabeth Leu, Patricia Bedame, Rosemary Lyons, Helen Kolonowski, Ruth Reichhardt* and *Irene Weglowski* during the last month.

The department extends a hearty welcome to *Theresa Gieser, Joseph McClelland* and *Homer R. McElroy* as the latest addition to our personnel.

Congratulations are extended to *Mr. Bert A. Hall* upon completion of 40 years of service. He was presented with a Sheaffer Pen and Pencil Set.

Ruth Johnson accompanied by her little daughter spent her vacation in Western Saskatchewan, Canada, visiting relatives and friends. With plenty of snow on the ground the highlight of her vacation was hitching old dobbin to the sleigh and going for a long ride.

Our deepest sympathy is extended to *Lucy Cramblet* in the loss of her brother who passed away on Monday, October 1, and also to *Olive Battersby* in the loss of her uncle who passed away on Saturday, October 13, 1945.

With the best wishes of the department, we are looking forward to the rapid recovery and welcome return of *Helen Dzien* who was remembered with "get well" cards, and a useful gift.

Lucy Cramblet who retired Wednesday, October 31 to live in Muskegon, Michigan.

By January 1945, it was apparent that it was just a matter of time until Germany was ultimately defeated and the same was true for Japan. As the nation began to anticipate the dawn of peace, so it was that events began to develop locally in Chicago regarding orders for additional modern streetcars and the long anticipated unification of Chicago's transit services under one management that would include the Chicago Surface Lines and the Chicago Rapid Transit Company. To that effect, the following significant events occurred in 1945:

March 3, 1945	The Federal Court authorized the Joint Board of Management and Operation of the Chicago Surface Lines to enter into contracts with specified manufacturers for 200 new streetcars and 195 buses.
April 12, 1945	Illinois Governor Dwight Green signed the Metropolitan Transit Authority Act which had been passed by the state legislature on April 5, 1945. This act created the Chicago Transit Authority which was assigned the responsibility of acquiring the properties of the Chicago Surface Lines and the Chicago Rapid Transit Company and operating these properties under a unified administration.
June 4, 1945	Chicago voters approved the Metropolitan Transit Authority Act in a local referendum.
October 17, 1945	Judge Michael L. Igoe, the federal court-appointed receiver for the Chicago Surface Lines, entered a court order authorizing the trustees of the CSL to spend up to $15,000,000 for transit equipment. The authorization included the purchase of an additional 400 PCC streetcars. This purchase was endorsed by the Chicago Transit Board which was not yet an operating entity.

The Postwar PCCs

So, by mid-October 1945 it appeared that the future for the modern PCC streetcar was going to be very bright in Chicago once the 600 new streetcars were delivered. CSL indicated it would assign the cars to four of its major trunk car lines, those being Clark-Wentworth with 182 cars, Broadway-State with 150 cars, Western Avenue with 171 cars, and 63rd Street with 75 cars. This assignment of new PCC cars was graphically illustrated in the map published in the October-November 1945 issue of *Surface Service* reproduced on the next page. Although this car allocation was devised in 1945, in reality the cars that were to be assigned to 63rd Street were instead allocated to Madison Street with the Madison Street "Blue Geese" in turn assigned to 63rd Street in 1948.

Following the direction of the Federal Bankruptcy Court, the CSL placed the following orders for postwar PCC streetcars:

March 1945	Pullman-Standard, 110 cars (Nos. 4062-4171), delivered 9/46-3/47
July 1945	St. Louis Car Company, 10 cars (Nos. 4052-4061), delivered 07/47-08/47
	St. Louis Car Company, 90 cars (Nos. 7035-7114), delivered 05/47-07/47
January 1946	St. Louis Car Company, 40 cars (Nos. 4372-4411), delivered 04/48-10/48
	St. Louis Car Company, 160 cars (Nos. 7115-7274), delivered 12/47-04/48
January 1946	Pullman-Standard, 200 cars (Nos. 4172-4371), delivered 09/47-03/48

Facing Page: Tiger stripes added to fronts of 1936 PCC cars to improve visibility. *Surface Service Magazine*, Oct-Nov 1945.
Wien-Criss Archive

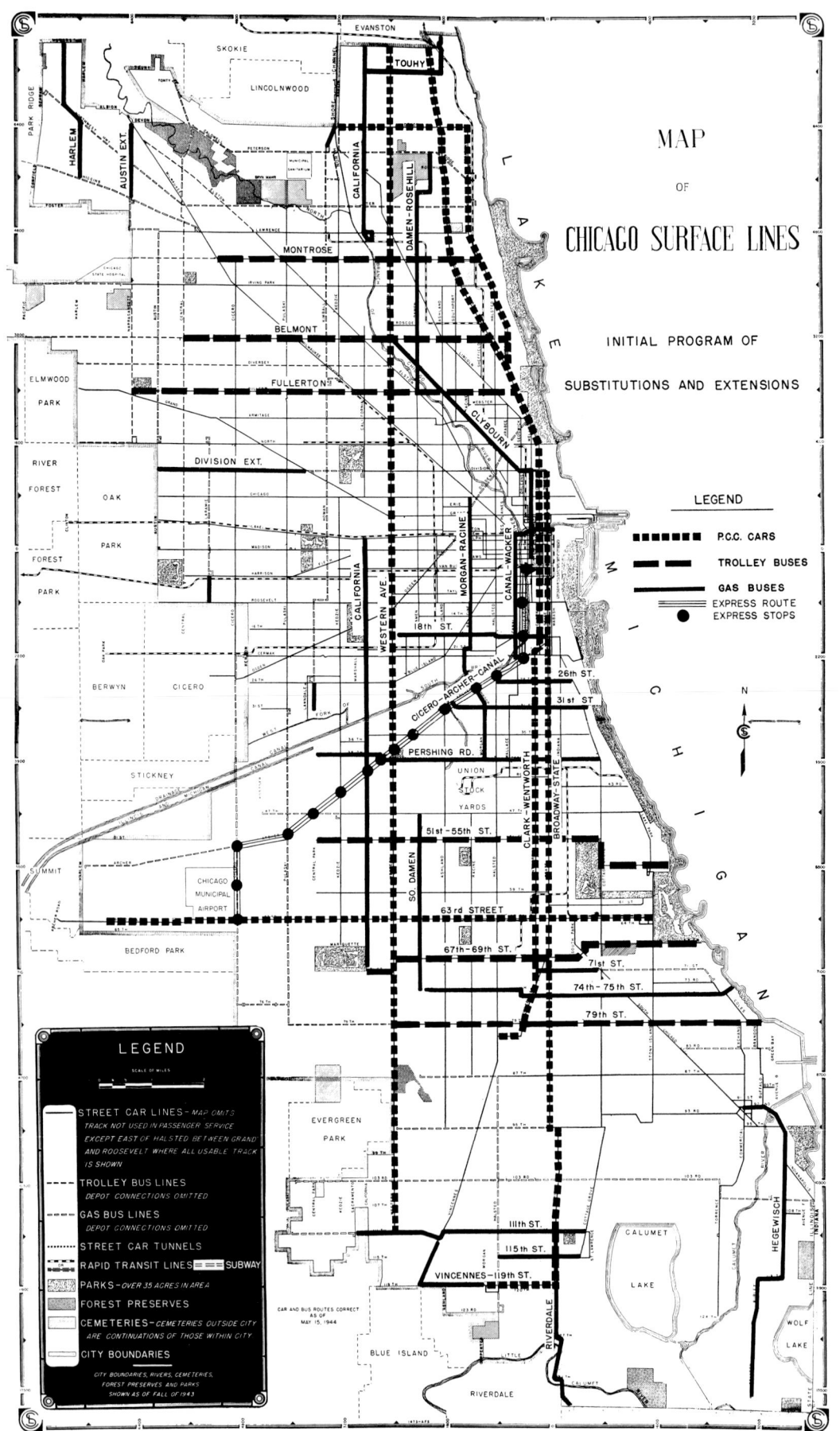

Chicago Surface Lines map showing planned PCC lines.
Surface Service, October-November 1945

Like the 1936 PCC streetcars that had operated on Madison Street, the postwar PCC streetcars were two-man cars with a motorman and a conductor; they were 50 feet in length and 9 feet wide; however unlike the earlier cars they were rear entrance rather than front entrance. It was believed that the rear entrance door arrangement provided faster loading and unloading of passengers than did the front entrance arrangement. The cost per car was $22,500 and it was estimated that the useful lives of the new cars were thirty years. When the last cars ordered were delivered in October 1948, the PCC streetcar fleet had reached a zenith of 683 vehicles. This was the largest fleet of PCC streetcars purchased new by any American city.

During 1945 and 1946, the Surface Lines placed ads in local newspapers proudly promoting the new PCC streetcars that were on order and later, after they began arriving, announcing to everyone the virtues of the new streetcars. The following pages contain examples of the ads that the Surface Lines placed in local publications in 1945 and 1946. Reproductions of the ads appeared in CSL's *Surface Service*.

The first production PCC car, number 4062, entered preview service on September 16, 1946, and was proudly touted by the CSL in the October 1946 issue of *Surface Service*.

continued on page 39

Car 4062 at Pullman-Standard Plant in Worcester, Massachusetts, ready to ship to Chicago in September 1946. *CERA Archives*

3 Views: Car 4062 preview at 78th and Vincennes on September 30, 1946.
John Bromley Collection

Pullman-Standard builder's plate.
Wien-Criss Archive

Car 4062 preview at 78th and Vincennes on September 30, 1946 showing location of Pullman-Standard builder's plate above motorman's seat.
Bernard L. Stone Photo

Coming—

395 NEW STREET CARS AND BUSES

Just as soon as Uncle Sam says the word, they'll be rushed into production for the convenience of Surface Lines' 4,000,000 daily riders.

Orders already have been placed for these 395 swift, modern conveyances... 195 of them gasoline buses, 200 street cars. In addition manufacturers are preparing bids on 100 trolley buses. All will be the last word in riding comfort.

Ever since 1941, your neighbors who operate CSL have been doing everything possible to obtain new equipment that would provide seats and speed service for our patrons. Some of these vehicles were ordered then. Others have been ordered just recently; still more are planned for; and it is our sincere hope that they will be greeting you at your regular street corner in the not too distant future.

Meanwhile, depend upon the men in CSL uniforms to leave nothing untried in their efforts to keep up the standard of present-day service in the face of wartime handicaps. More than 3000 street cars and buses are in service daily carrying Chicago's workers to their essential jobs. That's every vehicle we have the manpower to operate. True, some of them, under normal conditions, would have been retired long ago, but our workers behind the scenes are on the job extra hours and on rest days to keep these street cars and buses running until better equipment is available.

CHICAGO SURFACE LINES

CHICAGO'S CITY-WIDE   TRANSIT SERVICE

MEN NEEDED

It is pleasant to think of new streetcars and buses coming to Chicago. But men to run the present equipment is an even more urgent need.

APPLY TODAY—1165 N. CLARK, or any car station

Surface Service, June 1945

IT WON'T BE LONG NOW

195 BUSES, 200 STREET CARS BEING BUILT FOR CHICAGO SURFACE LINES

For years we have been wanting them, now they're really started. The Government has said, "O.K.", contracts have been let and production is under way on 395 of the swiftest, smoothest, safest street cars and buses that modern designers have been able to conceive.

This $6,559,665 contract is Surface Lines' start in creating a new standard of comfortable and convenient transportation for Chicago. Fourteen of the buses already have been delivered, more are expected this summer. Everything possible is being done to hurry the rest. Delivery on the street cars has been promised for late 1945 and early 1946.

During recent years, CSL service hasn't always been up to the standard we would like it to have been. It wasn't due to a lack of effort, however. Your neighbors in CSL uniforms have worked extra hours, often have given up days of rest, to keep transportation rolling. But wartime shortages have proved a serious handicap. With new equipment and more men to operate it, we're looking forward to the time when you can depend upon finding a street car or bus where you want it, when you want it.

MEN WANTED RIGHT NOW

Hundreds of conductors and trolley pilots are needed to keep present equipment running. It's an important job, for without transportation, war production is bound to lag. So enlist now in CSL and help get war-workers to the factories and home again. Steady work.

APPLY TODAY
1165 N. Clark Street
or any car station

 **CHICAGO SURFACE LINES**

CHICAGO'S CITY-WIDE TRANSIT SERVICE

Surface Service, August 1945

Arriving Now...

NEW BUSES NOW... NEW STREET CARS SOON

On Chicago's streets—today—are the first visible proofs of post-war promises come true!

Brand new buses—with latest improvements for speed, safety and comfort, are now being inducted into immediate Chicago Surface Lines service. Soon to follow are 200 modern streamlined street cars.

Yet these are only the first arrivals of a huge modern CSL fleet of conveyances designed to replace older transportation equipment.

They're the vanguard of *1275* new motor buses, trolley buses, and ultra-modern street cars that will be placed in daily service in all parts of Chicago.

These first arrivals are the practical realization of Surface Lines' first order for 195 new gasoline buses and 200 street cars. As we previously promised, they're the last word in safe riding comfort.

And—as they continue to arrive—they bring you further promise of 880 *more* units, already authorized for quickest possible production.

Take personal advantage of this new Surface Lines equipment—enjoy the convenience it affords you each day. But watch the *continued* improvement in CSL service—and enjoy each new benefit as each one is added in your immediate future.

CSL NEEDS ADDITIONAL MEN FOR STEADY PERMANENT WORK

We need more good men to keep CSL buses and street cars rolling. It's important work and steady work that offers rich opportunities for good earnings and future security. There are no pay deductions for such benefits as free hospitalization—life, accident and health insurance—and yearly 14 day vacations. We need you now, so see us today.

APPLY NOW, AT 1165 NORTH CLARK STREET

CHICAGO SURFACE LINES
CHICAGO'S CITY-WIDE TRANSIT SERVICE

Surface Service, December 1945

NOW IT'S ~~395~~ 1275 NEW BUSES AND STREET CARS

to help Chicagoans go places

Now CSL plans for sweeping city transit improvements have turned into actual realities! Approval has been granted for 880 additional new buses and street cars, which, with the 395 others already ordered, will add to the speed, convenience and comfort of transportation in all parts of the city.

This new equipment will make possible the conversion of 22 present street car lines to bus operations, the modernization of four heavily-traveled street car lines, the installation of a new express bus line and several extensions.

Chicagoans will be proud of these new motor buses, trolley buses, and modern streamlined street cars. All will incorporate the latest developments for safety, speed and riding ease. The new street cars will be of ultra-modern design in both body construction and smooth, "noiseless" operation.

Deliveries are already being made on the first part of this huge equipment order. Construction will proceed rapidly on this latest order, with delivery of all street cars and most of the buses scheduled for 1946.

Soon you will be able to say: "It's a pleasure to go places in Chicago on our Chicago Surface Lines!"

CHICAGO SURFACE ⓢ LINES

CHICAGO'S CITY-WIDE TRANSIT SERVICE

Surface Service, January 1946

CHICAGO SURFACE LINES
New Street Cars
NOW IN SERVICE

FOUR MORE MAJOR CSL ROUTES WILL BE COMPLETELY EQUIPPED WITH STREAMLINERS

Now running in regular service are the first of the new ultra-modern Chicago Surface Lines street cars. The world's finest in comfort, speed, safety and convenience, they are the visible fulfillment of CSL's promises to you!

The first of these cars are now running on the Clark-Wentworth route. Steadily—each week—as fast as deliveries are received, their number will grow until this important traffic line is completely equipped with these new streamliners.

Six hundred of these fast, smooth-rolling vehicles are scheduled for soon-as-possible delivery. Other lines which will be completely re-equipped, in addition to Clark-Wentworth (and Madison Street which already has streamliners) are Broadway-State, Western Avenue, and 63rd Street.

This CSL modernization program is the result of long and careful planning. Starting in March, 1945, these 600 new street cars, 465 new motor buses, and 210 trolley buses were ordered. Already over 200 of the buses are on duty, helping to extend and improve CSL routes, schedules and service.

WITH MORE NEW EQUIPMENT WE NEED MORE GOOD MEN!

We still need more men—men who want steady jobs—
—good jobs—whether times are good or bad—to help keep our buses and street cars rolling. It's important work with good pay and opportunity for permanent security. See us today.

APPLY NOW—At 1165 North Clark Street

CHICAGO SURFACE LINES
CHICAGO'S CITY-WIDE TRANSIT SERVICE

Surface Service, October 1946

Surface Service

OCTOBER, 1946

MEET CHICAGO'S SURFACE-LINER

Public Gets Preview of New Streamlined Streetcar

THE FIRST of 600 new modern streamlined streetcars arrived in the city early in September and was put on public exhibition on the opening day of the American Transit Association convention.

During the convention, the car was operated in the loop, providing free transportation for the public. Constructed in the Worcester, Massachusetts, plant of the Pullman Standard Car Manufacturing company, the car was the first delivered on orders for 600 placed in 1945 with the Pullman company and the St. Louis Car company.

Orders for the first 200 of the cars were approved by Judge Igoe in March,

These smooth green and cream colored cars will soon be a common sight on Chicago streets. . . . A new passenger convenience is the non-jam window mechanism which operates by a crank.

COVER: Prior to the public preview of CSL's new streamlined streetcar, the management and officers of the Chicago Surface Lines inspected the vehicle, accompanied by Federal Judge Michael L. Igoe, who has jurisdiction over the reorganization proceedings of the Surface Lines companies. . . . In the picture, left to right, are: Evan J. McIlraith, general manager; Charles H. Albers, trustee and board member; John E. Sullivan, chairman, Joint Board of Management and Operation; Federal Judge Michael L. Igoe; Edward J. Fleming, trustee and board member; and Thomas J. Friel, trustee and board member.

1945, and the balance last December. Purchase of the cars was in conformity with orders entered by the Illinois Commerce Commission.

Additional deliveries are scheduled at the rate of eight to ten a week during the fall. The Clark-Wentworth line will be the first equipped with the new cars. Other lines to get modern streetcars are Broadway-State, Western Avenue and 63rd Street.

The new cars are part of the Surface Lines post-war improvement program. Ordered in the last 18 months, also, were 465 motor buses and 210 trolley buses. The buses, of which 190 already have been delivered, are being used as part of an extensive program of extensions and substitutions for streetcars.

Like Madison Street

The new streetcar resembles in many respects the streamliners now operated on Madison street, but has numerous improvements in performance, appearance and comfort over that first model of the modern "P.C.C." car. Seating 58 passengers, it is even quieter than the Madison street model, due to further developments in springs and rubber cushionings. It is smoother in starting and stopping and can keep its place in traffic due to its fast acceleration.

The car is nine feet wide and 50 feet long, exceeding the present width of the Madison street car by 3 inches, with the gain being translated into a wider aisle. It is the longest and widest streetcar built in the country in recent years. Instead of air brakes and air mechanism for operation of doors, these controls are electrically operated.

The car is painted in the new Surface Lines color scheme adopted early this year for all of its new equipment. The

On the first day of the Public Preview, Station WMAQ did a news broadcast from the car. Instructor Bert Sayre (left) was interviewed by the announcer (center) and old-time motorman Eugene Devine (seated, right) of 77th told of the contrast with streetcars of the old days. . . . The interior of the vehicle is elegant with its pastel-colored walls, leather seats, wide, non-skid aisle and forced-air ventilating system.

SURFACE SERVICE

lower half of the body is a bright Mercury green and the upper part and roof, Croyden cream with a brilliant holly orange dividing stripe below the windows. The interior is in three shades of light blue-gray. Most seats face forward and are shaped and upholstered to give maximum comfort. They are covered with brown leather. Stanchions are used freely at convenient locations for passengers moving through the car. The stanchions rise from the grab handle at the top of the seat on the aisle side to the ceiling. There is a stanchion from every second seat.

Another improvement for the convenience of the passengers is the use of an easily operated window mechanism. Instead of the conventional latches, a non-jam automotive type of mechanism is used. The windows may be opened or closed readily by simply turning a crank directly above the center of the window.

No-Glare

A feature of the car is its "no-glare" windshield, a development since the Madison street cars were built. Its construction, combining slanted V-shaped windshield with a black shadow apron, eliminates glare from interior lighting, making for safety of night operation and doing away with the curtain behind the motorman. The clear view ahead at night is shared also by the passengers.

Fast acceleration and speed is assured by four high-speed motors. These motors have a large short-time overload capacity and drive the car axles through silent hypoid gearing. The car can accelerate at the rate of 4.75 miles per hour per second on level track.

The trucks on the cars are of a standardized construction for all modern

Free rides were given to all-comers as the car circled the Loop on its two-day Public Preview. . . . This convenient set-up will please every motorman. The control handle and magnetic track brake are on the operator's left. The brake handle is on his right, and on the floor is the reverse lever. Included on the dash are brake signal lights and an ampmeter, indicating if the car is in operable condition.

OCTOBER, 1946

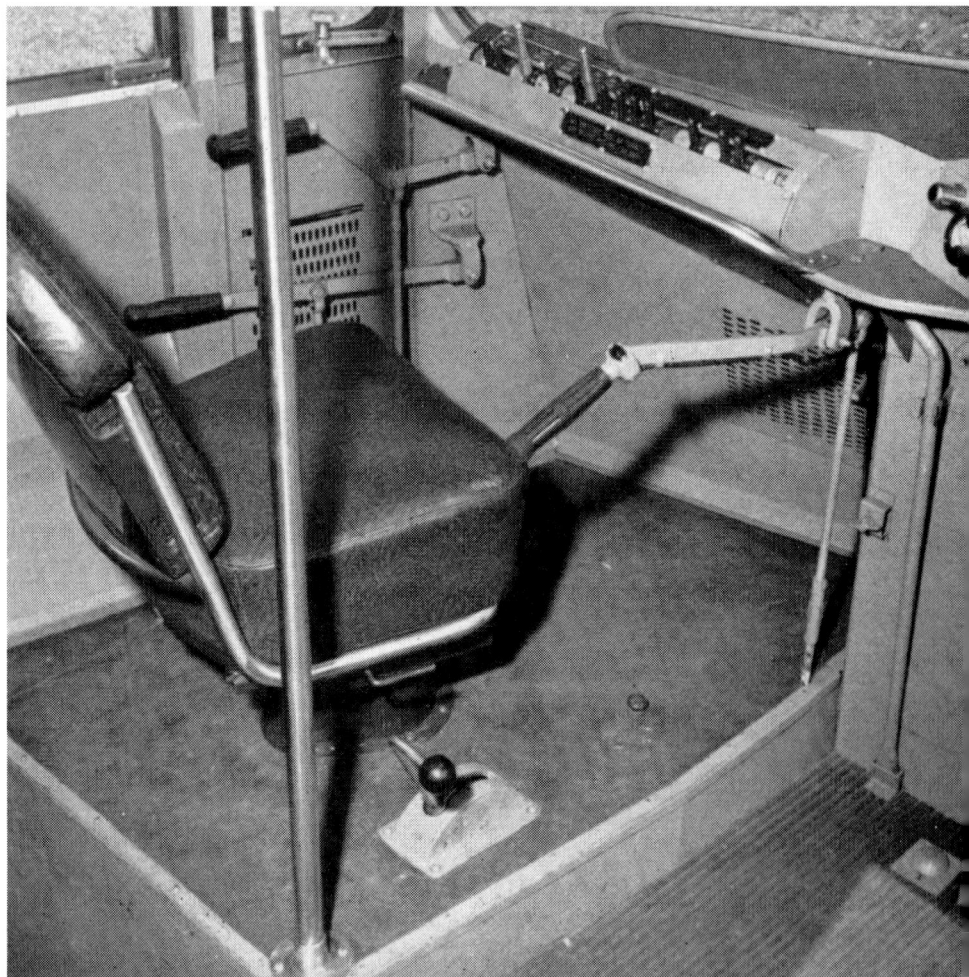

streetcars. It is through the quiet motors, hypoid gears and the use of rubber in wheel and truck construction that the greatest gain has been made in elimination of noise.

Wheels are of super-resilient design with the steel tire separated from the wheel hub by thick rubber cushions. The thickness of the rubber cushion is twice that used on the Madison street car.

The car is equipped with three independent braking systems—motor braking, spring-applied electric solenoid-release drum brakes, and electro-magnetic track brakes.

Motor braking is effective to give almost a complete stop. As the speed of the vehicle approaches zero, the spring drum brakes come into action and provide the braking to complete the stop, as well as the parking brake. In addition, to those two systems, battery-operated track brakes, in which energized magnets grab the rails, are always available either with or independent of the other brakes. There are four track brakes, one on each side of each truck.

Greater Comfort

Wider aisles, permitting smoother flow of passengers through the vehicles, "natural" steps, non-slip floor surface and maximum smoothness of operation all provide additional convenience and safety for passengers. "Standee" windows above the regular side windows will permit standing passengers to look out with ease.

Comfort for the passengers is enhanced by high intensity illumination and effective circulation of air by ventilation and heating. Heating, which is automatically controlled, is provided chiefly as a by-product of motor braking supplemented by auxiliary heaters.

The car has the motorman's controls at only one end and each car will have six pairs of doors, operated by electrical controls. It is a rear-entrance car with three pairs of doors at the rear for entering and one pair of doors at the center and two pairs at the front for exit.

"We Do Appreciate Courtesy"

OPERATOR HARRY LICHT—Lawndale.

"The driver noticed people getting off the streetcar on Central Park, and using very good judgment, waited to see if people were going to board his bus. I can't tell you how grateful we were for such service at that time of night. He just smiled and said that *it was his duty*. . . . Again I say much praise is due him," wrote Mrs. Jos. Lanzendorf, 2420 S. Lawndale, "for we of the public *do* appreciate courtesy."

Eighteen employes of Heymann-Malone and Associates, 179 W. Washington, also expressed their "appreciation of the courtesy, thoughtfulness and consideration of Harry Licht" during his early morning run.

OPERATOR HUGH GIBBONS—69th

"The extra service I received yesterday prompted," Mrs. Verna Larson, 8213 S. Ada to write. "Not only did he (Mr. Gibbons) enable me to catch his car, and was pleasant about it, but he practically lifted an elderly woman with a cane onto the car at the next intersection.

Mrs. E. A. Carlsten, 6840 Calumet, observed Gibbons get off his car and lead a little two year old girl out of the street, "and asked an older youngster to take the child home. By taking time to perform this courtesy . . . he saved a lot of grief as the trucks and cars speed up and down 69th very fast. He is doing his best to make the streets safe for all."

CONDUCTOR FRED STROM—Kedzie

Mrs. Mary Felthouse and Mrs. Jennie Gehrke, 8222 S. Ashland were present when Strom picked up a helpless cripple and carried him off the car to a place of safety—which caused them to remark that "a fellow like that's a credit to any place he works for."

MOTORMAN FRANK PACULA—Noble

Mr. Wm. L. Kevil, 416 N. Morgan, advises that as his wife got off the car late one night, "two men jumped off the car at the same time. The street was dark and no one was around. Conductor No. 7031 (Pacula) waited to see which way the two men went before he started his car. Thanks for his thoughtfulness."

CONDUCTOR WILLARD HOFFMAN—Cottage Grove

"The efficiency of this conductor was noticed, not only by myself, but many other passengers—his courtesy, and the assistance he rendered to aged people getting on and off was above anything I have seen," stated Mrs. Charles E. Kleinhans, 915 Webster.

MOTORMAN ARTHUR SCHOEN—Armitage

"He called out streets clearly and cautioned, very pleasantly, everyone leaving the car through the front door. I believe such performances as his make for good public relations," wrote J. F. Rice, 72 W. Adams.

CONDUCTOR JOSEPH MUTSCHINSKY—Limits

"I have yet to see a better workman, besides being a very polite and exacting conductor. You should be commended on hiring a man of this caliber, and more power to you in finding more of them."—Stephen Pincsak, 2646 N. Dayton

OPERATOR GEORGE SPORLEDER—Lawrence

Mrs. C. L. Wright, 5243 Lake, is handicapped by being blind, so she greatly appreciated the kindness of Sporleder when he conducted her from his bus to the waiting streetcar.

CONDUCTOR OTTO POTRATZ, and MOTORMAN ARTHUR ULLSTEAD—Limits

One of those muchly-to-be-appreciated commendations from a fellow-employe was earned by this crew when they voluntarily switched their direction to fill a gap in the street caused by an accident. Due to several relay trips which they ran, service was maintained just about normal.

So New

THEY'LL BE YEARS AHEAD FOR YEARS TO COME!

Clear vision ahead, with no night-time glare, is provided by new shadow-aproned slanted windshield.

50 feet long and 9 feet wide, with wider passages—more convenient entrances and exits.

NEW CSL STREET CARS ARE EVEN BETTER THAN YOU'VE EXPECTED!

Effortless control helps motorman avoid strain and fatigue, adds to safety and comfort of passengers.

Long, wide and handsome—the new CSL cars now taking their places on Chicago streets have numerous improvements on even the sleek Madison Street streamliners.

Seating 58 passengers, they are even more quiet, because of still further developments in springs and rubber cushionings. They are smoother in starting and stopping, yet have fast acceleration and positive, triple-brake action.

Wheels are of super-resilient design, with steel tire separated from the wheel hub by extra-thick cushions of rubber. Each car has four high speed motors that drive through silent hypoid gearing.

Here, in these new cars now entering actual service, are the finest engineering improvements—to help you go places in Chicago with greater convenience, comfort, safety and speed!

CSL NEEDS ADDITIONAL MEN FOR STEADY PERMANENT WORK

We need more good men to keep CSL buses and street cars rolling. These are good jobs in good times or bad. There are no pay deductions for such benefits as free hospitalization—life, accident and health insurance—and yearly 14 day vacations. We need you now, so see us today.

Apply Now, at 1165 North Clark Street

CHICAGO SURFACE LINES
CHICAGO'S CITY-WIDE TRANSIT SERVICE

(One of the advertisements prepared for the current series now appearing in Chicago papers.)

Surface Service, November 1946

FOR YOU!

New Comfort...
New Convenience

IN CHICAGO'S *NEW* CSL STREET CARS

New wider aisles, with stanchions at every second seat, improve the ease and safety of passenger movement through the car.

"Non-Jam" automotive type opening cranks are conveniently located directly above center of each window.

3 pairs of doors at the rear for entrance or exit and exit doors at center and at front, are all operated by electrical controls.

THESE ARE IMPROVEMENTS YOU WILL ENJOY IN CSL'S NEW MODERN LUXURY STREAMLINERS

Never before has it been possible to ride through the streets of Chicago with such comfort and convenience, at such little expense! Now—in the ultra-modern new CSL street cars rapidly being placed in service—Chicagoans will be a step ahead of the whole nation with faster, safer, and more comfortable city surface transportation!

Your comfort is enhanced by roomy seating capacity for 58 passengers—wider aisles—better ventilation, heating, and illumination. When standing, upper windows permit you to see street numbers and signs without stooping.

Most seats face forward and are shaped for comfortable relaxation. Upholstered in brown leather, they stay freer from soil and from dust.

For your convenience, entrances and exits are skillfully arranged, "natural" door steps are provided, and non-slip floor surfaces to further guard your safety.

All these new comforts and conveniences, coupled with the most advanced improvements in smooth, quiet operation, will give you every-day satisfaction when you go places in Chicago!

CSL NEEDS ADDITIONAL MEN FOR STEADY PERMANENT WORK

We need more good men to keep CSL buses and street cars rolling. These are good jobs in good times or bad. There are no pay deductions for such benefits as free hospitalization—life, accident and health insurance—and yearly 14 day vacations. We need you now, so see us today.

Apply Now, at 1165 North Clark Street

CHICAGO SURFACE LINES
CHICAGO'S CITY-WIDE TRANSIT SERVICE

(One of the advertisements prepared for the current series now appearing in Chicago papers.)

Surface Service, December 1946

CHICAGO

Chicago Transit Authority
enters fourth year of $150,000,000 program

From the start of the program in 1945 to the end of 1948, a total of $37,500,000 was spent for modernization of equipment and facilities.

NEW FLEET

As the year 1948 closed, 600 streamlined streetcars, 210 trolley coaches, 4 experimental "L"-subway cars and 900 buses had been placed in service. In addition, an order was placed for 130 Rapid Transit Cars—Chicago's first new fleet of elevated-subway equipment since 1925. Five principal lines have been equipped with modern PCC cars and four lines have been modernized with streamlined trolley coaches. By the end of 1955, CTA plans to have spent $152,374,300, and to have purchased 1000 new electric elevated and subway cars, 800 new streetcars and 2725 new trolley coaches and buses.

IMPROVEMENTS

Also proposed under this program are a modern signal system on the entire elevated-subway system, plant improvements such as new shops, garages, rehabilitation of elevated structures, *and a continuing policy of replacing worn-out and obsolete equipment with new vehicles.*

SELF-SUPPORTING

And the Chicago Transit Authority *cannot* depend upon public taxes. Although an autonomous public body making its own rules and regulations, the Chicago Transit Authority cannot levy a tax and so *must support itself out of revenues.*

MOVING PEOPLE

Here is an example of modern transit planning . . . with the aim of *moving people* rather than automobiles. Each vehicle is placed in its correct application. Rapid transit vehicles for long haul traffic, modern PCC cars for the heaviest of surface traffic, trolley coaches for less dense surface traffic, and buses for lighter lines and feeder service.

Mass Transportation Magazine ad, February 1949
CERA Archives

MODERNIZES A SYSTEM

Artist's sketch of the type of "L"-subway car ordered for Chicago's elevated and subway system. A total of 130 units were ordered. Speed and comfort are primary requirements.

Modern PCC cars carry the heaviest load of surface traffic in Chicago. Passengers find them fast, comfortable, quiet and odorless.

Heavy loading conditions don't stall traffic in Chicago where trolley coaches' wide double doors and roomy aisles speed passenger loading and discharging.

Modern transit should be planned as a system—with each vehicle in its proper traffic sphere. Electrics quickly gain the confidence of the riding public because they are fast, quiet, comfortable and roomy. They quickly gain the wholehearted approval of management because of their operating and maintenance economy...and their increased earning power.

Our transportation specialists are available to help you solve your transit problems. Call your nearest G-E office or write Apparatus Dept., General Electric Co., Schenectady, N. Y.

GENERAL ELECTRIC

KEEP IT BALANCED!
BULLETIN TO TRAINMEN

THE CROWDING OF PASSENGERS AT OR NEAR THE ENTRANCE CREATES A SERIOUS PROBLEM. EVERY TRAINMAN CAN HELP SOLVE IT.

CAR CARDS, OR STREAMERS, URGING PASSENGERS TO MOVE TO THE OPPOSITE END AFTER BOARDING ARE BEING PLACED IN OUR VEHICLES. TRAINMEN CAN HELP MAKE THEM EFFECTIVE. TO ACCOMPLISH RESULTS WILL REQUIRE TACT AND COURTESY.

TRY SAYING IN A PLEASANT MANNER, SOMETHING LIKE THIS:

"YOU'LL BE MORE COMFORTABLE AT THE OTHER END OF THE CAR"
OR
"IT ISN'T CROWDED FARTHER FRONT (OR BACK) IN THE CAR"

IF THE URGING ISN'T DONE PLEASANTLY, HOWEVER, IT MAY DO MORE HARM THAN GOOD.

INCIDENTALLY, COURTEOUS SERVICE AT ALL TIMES UNDER ALL CONDITIONS WILL MAKE THE JOB EASIER.

TRANSIT IS VITAL TO VICTORY

W. A. HALL,
SUPERINTENDENT OF TRANSPORTATION.

AGAIN...WE *Congratulate* CHICAGO!

AGAIN YOU ARE ONE OF THE **FIRST** TO GET THE LATEST IMPROVEMENTS IN MODERN CITY TRANSPORTATION

From the production lines of the St. Louis Car Company—the birthplace of today's modern streamlined street car—a steady stream of these fast, safe and luxuriously comfortable new vehicles is rolling into the service of your Chicago Surface Lines.

For ten years "St. Louis Built" streamliners have set new standards of service on the CSL Madison Street line. The Surface Lines was a pioneer in the introduction of these streamliners, being one of the first systems to give its passengers the startling new advantages of smooth and noiseless operation.

Now, CSL is among the first to receive deliveries of St. Louis Car Company's newest and even finer post-war models.

Today these new "St. Louis Built" CSL streamliners contain engineering advancements and improvements that will keep them years ahead for years to come. Use them, and enjoy them, whenever you want to "go places" in Chicago.

SINCE 1936,

WHEN THE FIRST "STREAMLINER" WAS BUILT BY THE ST. LOUIS CAR COMPANY, MODERN "ST. LOUIS BUILT" STREET CARS HAVE BEEN PLACED IN SERVICE IN:

Chicago	Los Angeles
Brooklyn	Minneapolis
Baltimore	Philadelphia
Cleveland	Pittsburgh
Cincinnati	St. Louis
Detroit	San Diego
Kansas City	San Francisco
Washington	Johnstown

Watch the fleet of "St. Louis Built" Streamliners GROW!

St. Louis Car Company
St. Louis, Mo.

MORE IMPROVEMENTS—Recently when the Chicago Surface Lines received the first of the 290 new streamlined streetcars which it has on order with the St. Louis Car company, that concern announced the fact with the above advertisement, which appeared in various Chicago newspapers. . . . Almost identical in appearance and operation with the 110 Surface-Liners received from the Pullman Standard company during the past six months, the cars are being put into service as rapidly as they are received. . . . There are 200 more streetcars on order with the Pullman company, making a total of 600 cars already delivered or on order for 1947 delivery. . . . The interior color scheme in this new series is a combination of three tones of tan.

Surface Service, May 1947

Map of Streetcar Lines (as of 1950)

Once the new streetcars arrived on the property, they were put into service as quickly as possible so older equipment that had been running for many decades could finally be retired. Most of the Surface Lines promotional material focused on the cars manufactured by Pullman-Standard.

However, in the May 1947 issue of *Surface Service*, CSL featured an ad that the St. Louis Car Company had placed in transit trade journals promoting the new Surface Lines streamliners that it had manufactured. Just as the 1936 PCC cars had been given the moniker "Blue Geese," the postwar cars came to be nicknamed "Green Hornets" after the CTA took over streetcar operations in October 1947. As to why the postwar cars received the "Green Hornets" tag, the only theory that has ever been put forward with some credence is because the cars were painted green and were as fast as hornets.

This post-war public relations photo shows the interior of a PCC focusing on the automobile-style cranks for the "standee" windows.
Wien-Criss Archive

During 1946 and 1947, representatives of the Chicago Transit Authority (CTA) met with representatives of the receivers for the Chicago Surface Lines and Chicago Rapid Transit Company to work out what they felt were favorable terms for the sale of assets of the two entities to the CTA. During that period of time arrangements had to be made for the sale of bonds to finance the purchase of the properties by the CTA.

The CTA Modernization Plan

On May 27, 1947, the CTA board adopted a transit modernization program for the period 1947 to 1955. This program provided for the purchase of 800 PCC streetcars.

On June 27, 1947, Walter J. McCarter of the Cleveland Transit System was appointed General Manager of the CTA by the CTA board. He officially took office on August 5, 1947, when the CTA's bonds were officially sold to acquire the assets of CSL and CRT. On September 30, 1947, payment was made by the CTA to the trustees of the Chicago Surface Lines and the Chicago Rapid Transit Company for their properties. On October 1, 1947, the CTA officially took over operation of these properties and the surface and rapid transit operations were now under one management.

It is reported that General Manager Walter J. McCarter announced in November 1947 that the CTA was continuing to accept delivery of the new PCC streetcars because the CTA had been unsuccessful in annulling the contracts with Pullman-Standard and the St. Louis Car Company. The November 12, 1947 *Chicago Tribune* reported McCarter as saying that CTA would take delivery on the remainder of the postwar PCC order because "part of the order has been delivered and the remainder could not be cancelled without penalty."

The same issue of the *Tribune* reported:

"Shortly after becoming general manager of the Chicago Transit authority, Walter J. McCarter remarked that as long as he holds his position he will not recommend the purchase of any more street cars for Chicago. He is convinced the future of local transportation lies with rubber tired vehicles.

...the street car's greatest advantage is in the load it can carry. It seats 54 passengers as compared to the 36 or 44 on a motor or trolley bus.

Car 4318 loaded on a flatcar at 78th and Vincennes awaiting shipment to the St. Louis Car Company in October 1953.
William C. Hoffman Photo/Wien-Criss Archive

Car 7142 with electric locomotive L-201 prepared to ship to the St. Louis Car Company in May 1958.
William C. Hoffman Photo/Wien-Criss Archive

This was likely the chief consideration that caused Surface Lines officials, and later McCarter, to accept street cars for routes such as Madison st., Clark-Wentworth, and Broadway-State.

This advantage is regarded by McCarter as a temporary one which cannot save the street car, with its heavy investment in rails, inflexibility, noise, middle of the street loading, and interference with other traffic, from giving way to buses.

One of the reasons for McCarter's belief that street cars must go is based on the potential capacity of the city's rapid transit system (the subway and elevated trains). The largest item in the authority's 150 million dollar program is earmarked for improving this system.

The hoped for result is that the demands on surface carriers, which threaten to choke traffic movements hopelessly, will be diminished. This, in turn, would eliminate the chief reason for retaining street cars. In McCarter's view the ideal way to handle huge volumes of passengers is thru a system of feeder buses carrying passengers to swiftly moving Rapid Transit lines.

If McCarter's present plans are realized the Rapid Transit lines will operate only limited and express trains. Buses will replace the local services thus terminated."

The September 22, 1952, *Tribune*, in an article detailing the CTA's accomplishments in the previous three years under Chairman Ralph Budd, noted:

"The biggest change is the rapid replacement of street cars with free-wheeling rubber tire vehicles- the motor and trolley buses. In two or three years, only three routes are expected to be left in Chicago's once expansive web of street car trackage.

In addition to the CTA chairman, Budd, the No. 2 keyman in directing these vast changes is Walter J. McCarter, the transit authority's general manager. And altho each has produced many new ideas aimed at improving service, they are in general only carrying out a blueprint that was drafted 15 years ago.

This blueprint, known as the "Green Book" in local transit circles, was laid out by three men- the late Philip Harrington, former city traction expert; Maj. R. F. Kelker Jr., former engineer of the city council committee on local transportation, and Charles E. DeLeuw, partner in the engineering firm of DeLeuw Cather & Co.

At the direction of the late Mayor Kelly, these three drew up the basic plans for rejuvenating Chicago's deteriorated and bankrupt transit operations. Six failures to reorganize the old private companies with private capital resulted in the establishment of the CTA in 1945 by state law, a city ordinance, and a referendum.

A year before the CTA began actual operations, McCarter was hired from the Cleveland Transit company to "rubberize" Chicago's traction operations and help carry out the other changes because he had effected similar improvements for Cleveland."

To those in the transit industry it was no surprise that McCarter took a negative view of the new PCC streetcars that were arriving daily in Chicago. After all, he was recognized as being a proponent of the motor bus in large urban centers. Just as Guy Richardson had espoused the pro-streetcar philosophy of the CSL in 1936, so did Walter J. McCarter espouse the pro-motor bus philosophy of the CTA in 1947. It was McCarter's goal to completely remove all streetcars from the streets of Chicago—no matter how old or new they were—as quickly as possible. However, with a capital investment of $13,500,000 in virtually new streetcars with useful lives of thirty years, it would be no easy task to quickly replace them simply because McCarter and his staff preferred to operate motor buses.

Car 4173 and other stripped car bodies in St. Louis scrapyard in November 1953.
Raymond DeGroote Photo

Car 4173 and other stripped car bodies in St. Louis scrapyard in August 1954.
Richard C. Cerne Photo/CERA Archives

McCarter did not have any problem ordering hundreds of motor buses in the late 1940s and early 1950s, to retire the old red streetcars that had been plying the streets of Chicago for as many as forty or more years. However, the removal of the Green Hornets from the streets was a much more challenging task. After all, the CTA was a quasi-governmental body and as such was much more subject to public scrutiny than the privately-owned Chicago Surface Lines. To be successful in eliminating the fleet of modern streetcars, McCarter and his staff had to devise a methodology that financial analysts and the public would accept as being financially viable and rational.

The concept of preserving electrically-powered vehicles that were environmentally friendly was still some twenty-five to thirty years in the future. In the early 40s and 50s, environmental concerns about "clean air" were not something that transit operators generally considered when they were "modernizing" their operations. In fairness to McCarter and his staff, one has to acknowledge that the conversion from "rail to rubber" was not unique to Chicago during this period. Most American cities were replacing streetcars with motor and trolley buses at this time; some might even say that it was the "conventional wisdom" of the time.

At the same time McCarter was challenged with modernizing the surface fleet, he had a similar challenge in trying to modernize the Rapid Transit fleet that included hundreds of wooden cars, some of which dated back to the late nineteenth century. Starting in 1950 and 1951, the CTA took delivery of 200 new "L" cars which were dubbed "Green Hornet" PCC rapid transit cars.

They were manufactured by the St. Louis Car Company, the same company that had manufactured 290 Green Hornet streetcars. The technology of the Green Hornet streetcars had been adapted to the rapid transit by CTA's staff engineers working with the St. Louis Car Company. However, after the delivery of the Green Hornet rapid transit cars in 1951, there were still hundreds of antiquated wood "L" cars in service in need of replacement.

It was at this time that McCarter approached the Engineering Department of the CTA to ascertain if it might be feasible to make new PCC rapid transit cars out of components taken from the virtually new PCC streetcars that he wanted to replace with buses. Thus it was that the CTA board awarded contracts to Pullman-Standard and the St. Louis Car Company in October 1952 to test the practicality of salvaging parts from the PCC streetcars to be used in new PCC rapid transit cars. If the tests were successful, the major benefits that the CTA felt would be achieved would be: (1) the modernization of the rapid transit fleet would be accelerated; (2) the unit cost of converted PCC streetcars would be less than totally new rapid transit cars; and (3) the conversion policy of PCC streetcars into PCC rapid transit cars would permit the replacement of the new streetcars with motor buses without the public outcry that might occur if vehicles with thirty-year operational lives were to be retired after less than ten years of service.

Car 4263 loaded on a flatcar at 78th and Vincennes awaiting shipment to the St. Louis Car Company in September 1953.
George Krambles Photo/Krambles-Peterson Archive

The first inkling of a PCC Conversion Program came in late 1952, only a few months after top CTA officials had publicly stated the need to buy another 300 PCCs to complete the modernization

6000 series rapid transit cars manufactured with component parts from PCC streetcars at Halsted Street on the Englewood Branch in July 1954.
William C. Hoffman Photo/Wien-Criss Archive

Single unit rapid transit car manufactured with component parts from PCC streetcars at the Howard Street station of the Evanston line in May 1961.
Jeffrey L. Wien Photo/Wien-Criss Archive

6000 series rapid transit cars manufactured with component parts from PCC streetcars operating on the Congress Street line at Austin Avenue in March 1971.
Jeffrey L. Wien Photo/Wien-Criss Archive

Car 7142 loaded on a flatcar at 78th and Vincennes awaiting shipment to the St. Louis Car Company in May 1958.
Thomas H. Desnoyers Photo/Krambles-Peterson Archive

program (200 more per the 1947 Modernization Plan, and another 100 no doubt to permit retirement of the prewar PCCs):

"Plan to Convert Streetcars to Elevated Coaches"
(from a CTA employee newsletter, November-December 1952)

CONTRACTS were awarded October 10 by Chicago Transit Board to Pullman-Standard Car Company of Chicago and the St. Louis Car Company of St. Louis for building two sample rapid transit cars out of "Green Hornet" type streetcars. Both of these concerns built modern PCC streetcars for CTA. They were developed in a manner similar to the present undertaking.

This is the initial step to test the practicability of salvaging years of useful life in these "Green Hornets" which can be replaced by buses on surface routes. CTA now operates 200 of the latest type all-metal rapid transit cars.

If these test conversions are successful, these major benefits will be obtained:
1. Modernization of rapid transit cars will be speeded up.
2. The unit cost of converted cars, having as much useful life as completely new units, would be substantially less than for entirely new units.
3. The CTA will be able to meet the mandatory requirement, at a substantial saving in cost, to have an additional fleet of all-metal rapid transit cars ready for operation when the

Indiana Harbor Belt diesel 410 pulling flatcars containing two PCC cars one of which contains car 4336 in March 1954 for shipment to the St. Louis Car Company.
Bernard A. Rossbach Photo

NEW BUS SERVICE

- **CERMAK**
- **HALSTED**
- **HALSTED-DOWNTOWN**
- **KEDZIE-CALIFORNIA**
- **and LAKE**

SURFACE ROUTES

Effective May 30, 1954

CHICAGO TRANSIT AUTHORITY

SUBSTITUTION of buses for streetcars on May 30, 1954, on five CTA Surface routes marks the end of Chicago's old red streetcar lines.

In this latest modernization move, a total of 185 red cars, most of which have been in operation for nearly half a century, will be replaced by 235 buses on the Cermak, Halsted, Halsted-Downtown daytime service, Kedzie-California and Lake routes. For some time buses have been operating weekends on both the Halsted and Kedzie lines, and on Saturdays on the Halsted-Downtown line.

Approximately 298,000 weekday riders on these lines will benefit from the smooth-riding, rubber-tired, noise-proofed equipment, operated with less waiting time between vehicles than under the streetcar schedules. The buses will follow substantially the same routes as the streetcars, with the exception of Lake Street. Route details follow:

CERMAK

East and west in Cermak Road between a terminal in the vicinity of 47th Avenue, Cicero, on the west, and a terminal at Prairie Avenue on the east. On a typical weekday, about 20,500 riders patronize this line.

HALSTED

North and south in Halsted Street between 79th Street on the south and Waveland Avenue on the north. Approximately 108,000 riders on a typical weekday are served by the Halsted and Halsted-Downtown lines.

HALSTED-DOWNTOWN

North in Halsted to Archer, northeast to Clark, north to Dearborn, north to Polk, east to Clark, south to Archer, southwest to Halsted, and south to 79th Street. This is a daytime service only, Mondays through Saturdays.

KEDZIE-CALIFORNIA

North in Kedzie from 63rd Place to Chicago, east to California, north to Roscoe, and then back to 63rd over the same route. About 55,000 patrons are served daily by this line.

LAKE

East in Lake Street from a west terminal at Austin Boulevard to an east terminal at State St., then south to Randolph, west to Franklin, north to Lake and west to Austin. Eastbound from Austin to Pine buses will operate in Lake Street south of the railroad tracks. Westbound from Pine to Austin they will operate in Lake Street north of the railroad tracks.

This new routing is an extension of service from Clinton Street to State Street. Streetcar service terminated at Clinton Street. Now direct transfer connections will be provided with elevated, subway and surface routes in the Loop area, thus substantially adding to the convenience of the Lake Street service for approximately 14,500 daily riders.

Four Streetcar Lines Remain

WITH the conversion of these five lines, there will be only four streetcar routes in the CTA system -- Western Avenue, Clark-Wentworth, Broadway-State and Cottage Grove. These four lines are equipped with modern, noise-proofed "Green Hornet" streetcars.

Progress of Modernization

WHEN the CTA started as an operating organization on October 1, 1947, in excess of 3,200 streetcars, most of them the old red type, were in use on Chicago's streets. The old "reds," after nearly 50 years, have been disappearing from the Chicago transit scene in recent years. With this latest change, none of them will be scheduled for regular service, but some will be held in reserve for emergency use to supplement the modern fleet of cars when necessary.

Approximately 385 streamlined "Green Hornet" streetcars will provide regular service on the remaining streetcar lines. Altogether, CTA has invested more than $90,000,000 in streamlined cars and buses, and in modernizing other facilities since the start of its modernization program.

CTA's bus service flier detailing the changes to 8 Halsted and 42 Halsted-Downtown streetcar routes, May 1954. *Wien-Criss Archive*

rapid transit facility in the Congress Street superhighway is available for use, sometime within the next two to three years.

Under the provisions of CTA's franchise ordinance with the City of Chicago, only all-metal cars may be assigned to the Garfield Park rapid transit route when it begins operating in the median strip of the Congress Street superhighway.

Between 300 and 400 "Green Hornet" streetcars may be adapted to rapid transit operation if the test conditions meet expectations.

6000 series rapid transit cars manufactured with component parts from PCC streetcars at the Western Avenue station of the Milwaukee Avenue line in March 1971.
Jeffrey L. Wien Photo/Wien-Criss Archive

This attempt to convert the body shells of two PCC streetcars into a rapid transit car directly was unsuccessful, in part due to differences in floor height. You can read more about this on pages 22-29 of CERA Bulletin 115, *Chicago's Rapid Transit, Volume II: Rolling Stock/1947-1976.*

As a result of the contract, PCC car 4381 was sent to the St. Louis Car Company and car 4394 was sent to Pullman-Standard. Both cars were shipped to the car builders in October 1952. Based upon the tests at the two manufacturers, it was determined that the conversion from PCC streetcars to PCC rapid transit cars could be effected using the trucks, electric traction motors, electrical components, seats, stanchions, and window mechanisms from the scrapped streetcars.

Chicago's PCCs were non-standard and had dimensions that made them unsuitable for use in many other cities. The value of a used standard PCC in the 1950s averaged around $3,000-5,000 with a scrap value of much less than that.

CTA's challenge was to get the PCCs off the books while realizing a return equal to their depreciated value. For amortization purposes, CTA assumed they had a useful life of only 20 years. This compares to a 12-year life for contemporary buses. The postwar PCCs had cost $22,500 each,

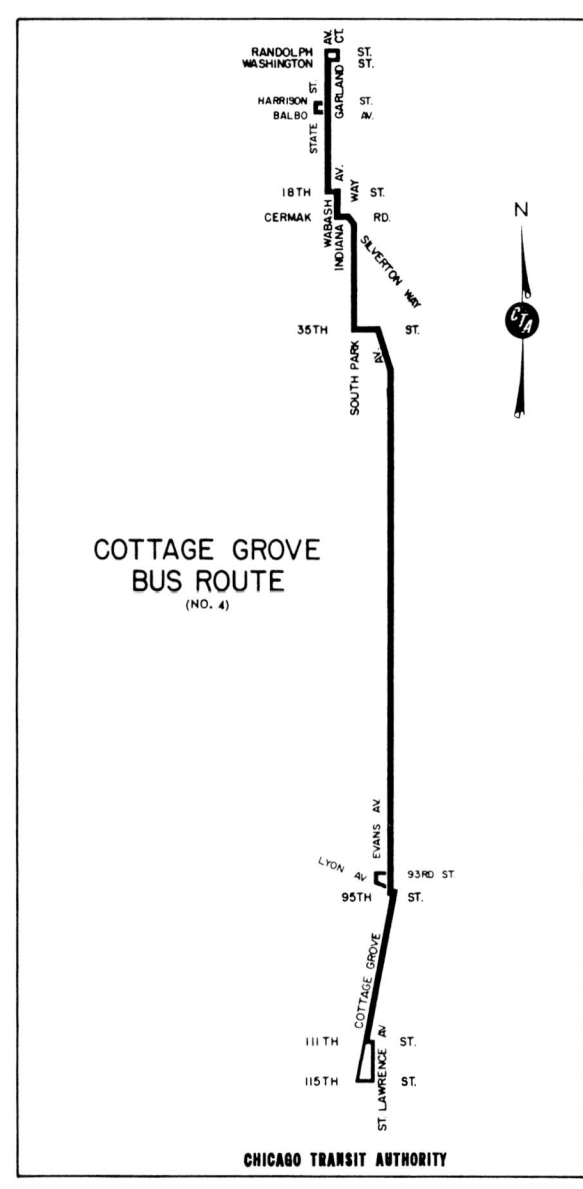

SERVICE CHANGES ON COTTAGE GROVE LINE
(ROUTE NO. 4)

EFFECTIVE JUNE 19, 1955

THE CLOSING of Cottage Grove Avenue, between 35th Street and 31st Street, for the privately-owned Lake Meadows housing project is requiring a change in the routing of the Cottage Grove Avenue line and the substitution of buses on the route for one-man streetcars. The changeover becomes effective on Sunday, June 19, 1955.

CHANGES IN THE LOOP

In the Downtown Loop, Cottage Grove Avenue buses, under the new arrangement, are scheduled to operate both north and south in Wabash Avenue, instead of north in State Street and south in Wabash Avenue, to a terminal at Garland Court and Randolph Street.

CHANGES SOUTH OF THE LOOP

Instead of operating in Cottage Grove Avenue between 35th Street and Cermak Road, the new routing for Cottage Grove Avenue buses is over South Parkway and Silverton Way, entering and leaving the Loop by way of Cermak Road, Indiana Avenue, 18th Street and Wabash Avenue.

SOUTH TERMINAL

The south terminal of the through service remains at 115th Street and Cottage Grove Avenue, with short-loop terminals established at 93rd Street and Cottage Grove Avenue on the south and at Harrison Street and Wabash Avenue on the north.

SCHEDULES

The new schedule provides service on weekdays at a two-minute interval in rush hours north of 95th Street and at four-minute intervals south of 95th Street; at a five-minute headway in the base period north of 95th Street and at a ten-minute headway south of 95th Street; and at a six-minute headway in the evening throughout the length of the route.

CHICAGO TRANSIT AUTHORITY
(SEE MAP ON REVERSE SIDE)

Service change flier from June of 1955 explaining the change from streetcars to motor buses on the 4 Cottage Grove line.
Wien-Criss Archive

and were therefore depreciating on the books at the rate of just over $1,000 per year. Once the 83 prewar PCCs approached 20 years of age in 1956, they were fully depreciated, and CTA promptly scrapped all except car 4021, retained as part of their historical collection.

Before the end of 1952, CTA realized that their original plan to convert PCC streetcars directly into rapid transit cars was unworkable. So, the plan then became to scrap the PCC body shells and reuse as many parts as possible in a new rapid transit car similar to the first 200 6000-series cars, which were made with all new parts. There were some differences between the two fleets--for example, the earlier cars had flat doors, while the rebuilds would have curved ones.

CTA decided to scrap the 310 Pullman PCCs first, and offered somewhat conflicting statements as to why. On the one hand, they said that the Pullmans had been less successful in use. On the other hand, they said that they had higher-quality parts that would be advantageous to use in rapid transit cars. Perhaps both statements are true. The Pullmans were heavier cars with better riding quality, but this probably resulted in a higher amount of electricity used, and increased operating cost over the 290 St. Louis-built cars. They were also the oldest postwar PCCs, with the most depreciation.

Having established that the conversion of PCC streetcars to PCC rapid transit cars was viable, McCarter energetically pursued his conversion program. CTA asked for bids on converting parts from PCC streetcars into rapid transit cars.

In late 1952 it was announced that the St. Louis Car Company was the low bidder over Pullman-Standard. The Pullman bid was $5,000 higher than St. Louis',s and was therefore considered non-competitive by CTA. Pullman did not bid on any subsequent PCC conversion orders.

On February 24, 1953, the CTA board authorized an order with the St. Louis Car Company for the building of 150 PCC rapid transit cars with an option for 100 additional cars. The first PCC streetcar, number 4173, a 1946 Pullman-Standard product, was shipped to St. Louis on May 28, 1953. It had seen less than seven years of service on the streets of Chicago. From that point on until March 1958, the CTA board entered into ongoing conversions contracts with the St. Louis Car Company until a total of 570 of the 600 postwar PCC streetcars had been sent to St. Louis for conversion.

Although the St. Louis Car Company had originally agreed to pay CTA $22,500 for each postwar PCC car, a figure which has been extensively quoted over the years, this contract was quickly cancelled, when it became apparent that conversion was not as simple a matter as it first appeared. In fact, as CTA reported in their 1961 Annual Report, the St. Louis Car Company paid CTA $14,000 for each of the 570 PCC streetcars.

In turn, there were additional costs involved in reconditioning parts, and these costs rose over the five years of the conversion program, as the parts had received more use. For another thing, it cost $3,000 to adapt the control equipment for each car.

By the end of the conversion program, these additional costs, which were added to the amount paid to St. Louis Car Co. for each of the 570 new "L"/subway cars, meant CTA received less revenue for each PCC streetcar turned in over time. By 1958, the net gain from each car was hardly more than scrap value.

The conversion program ended while CTA still had more than two dozen PCC streetcars left. With the Congress Expressway median line set to open, CTA's attentions turned to the development of high-speed rapid transit car motors. The idea had caught on with the public that a rapid transit car, traveling in a highway median, should be able to go at least as fast as the automobiles around it. CTA's high-speed experiments, which began in 1955, culminated in the 2000-series rapid transit cars built by Pullman in 1964, the forerunners of today's fleet.

**MODERN BUSES REPLACE
STREETCARS ON
WESTERN AVENUE**
(Route No. 49)
Effective June 17, 1956

EFFECTIVE Sunday, June 17, 1956, the one-man streetcars on Western Avenue disappear from that line, being replaced by modern buses.

This conversion from streetcars to buses will clear the way for the City of Chicago to proceed with its program of building vehicular traffic grade separations in heavily used Western Avenue intersections as well as repaving of the street.

The bus route remains the same as the streetcar route, with schedules being substantially the same. Buses will operate between the present north terminal at Berwyn and Western Avenues and the existing south terminal at 79th Street and Western Avenue, thereby retaining the functional characteristics of the route that prevent delays in traffic-congested areas from impairing the regularity of service on the outer reaches of Western Avenue.

The major difference under the new arrangement is that passengers will board and alight at the curb where bus stop zones will be established.

(See map on reverse side.)

CHICAGO TRANSIT AUTHORITY

**WESTERN AVENUE
BUS ROUTE NO. 49**
MAJOR TRANSFER POINTS

BERWYN LOOP 5300N

WESTERN AVE. STA.
RAVENSWOOD "L"
4700N-2400W

WESTERN AVE. STA.
LOGAN SQ. "L"
1900N-2400W

WESTERN AVE. STA.
DOUGLAS "L"
2032S-2400W

FOSTER 5200N
IRVING PARK 4000N
BELMONT 3200N
ARMITAGE 2000N
DIVISION 1200N
MADISON
ROOSEVELT 1200S
CERMAK 2200S
ARCHER 3800S
51ST. STREET
63RD. STREET

79TH. STREET LOOP

The Chicago Transit Aurthority's service change flier for the 49 Western streetcar route's conversion to motor buses in 1956.
Wien-Criss Archive

Better Service

The long Broadway-State route has been unwieldly since street traffic congestion became a major problem. Chronic service irregularities northbound in Broadway and southbound in State have been characteristic of the route.

With two, separate, shorter routes, service delays resulting from traffic congestion can be more easily overcome or compensated by spacing adjustments.

Service regularity, therefore, will be substantially improved on the outer ends of these two, new, shorter routes.

Alternate Services Available

For the comparatively few through riders who have been using the Broadway-State route, alternate services are available. The North-South fast "L"-Subway route, with its new, modern equipment, is conveniently accessible. So is the Clark-Wentworth streetcar route (No. 22) for riders who have been transferring to the Broadway-State route from east-west surface routes.

For Improved Service...

BROADWAY-STATE ROUTE REVISIONS

EFFECTIVE SUNDAY, DECEMBER 4, 1955

CHICAGO TRANSIT AUTHORITY

BROADWAY-STATE ROUTE REVISIONS

To improve service, including better adherence to schedules, Broadway-State (No. 36), Chicago's longest streetcar route, approximately 25 miles from end to end, is being divided into two routes, effective Sunday, December 4, 1955.

The two routes are: State Street (Route No. 36A) and Broadway (Route No. 36).

STATE STREET—ROUTE NO. 36A

This route will extend from State & Grand on the north to 119th & Morgan on the south. It will operate via State, 95th, Michigan, 119th, Morgan, 120th, Halsted and 119th back to Michigan and then north over the southbound route to Wacker Drive, east to Wabash, north to Grand, west to State, south to the terminal at 119th & Morgan.

A fleet of 71 LP-gas (odorless propane) buses, all 51-passenger units, will replace the 55 streetcars now necessary to operate the south part of the present Broadway-State route.

Improved Frequency

Service frequency will be improved to approximately two-minute intervals in rush hours, with four and four and one-half-minute and six-minute intervals being provided in the mid-day and evening hours, respectively. Owl service will operate at 15-minute intervals between Grand & State and 84th & State, and at 30-minute intervals between 84th & State and 119th & Morgan.

Board Buses at Safety Island

Please board State Street (No. 36A) buses, northbound and southbound, at the safety islands in the Loop area.

Other CTA buses stopping at the safety islands in the Loop are: Northbound, Archer Express (Route No. 62A), Michigan-State-Wacker shuttle (Route No. 149) and Wilson-Michigan (Route No. 153). Southbound, Michigan-State-Wacker (Route No. 149), Division (Route No. 70).

Loop Transfer Points

Passengers are permitted to transfer from Broadway (No. 36), southbound, to a State Street bus (No. 36A), southbound, at State & Grand, State & Lake, State & Monroe, or at State & Polk.

Passengers are permitted to transfer from a northbound State Street bus to the Broadway line at State & Polk, State & Monroe, or have the privilege of walking to Dearborn & Monroe to transfer.

Passengers desiring to ride northbound on the Broadway line may board southbound from Monroe to Polk, or board northbound Broadway streetcar (bus on week-ends and Holidays) on Dearborn.

BROADWAY—ROUTE NO. 36

Broadway will continue as a streetcar route, operating between Devon & Clark on the north and State & Polk on the south via Devon, Broadway, Clark, Division, State, Polk, Dearborn and Kinzie back to State and then north over the in-bound route.

Patrons in the Loop desiring northbound Broadway (Route No. 36) service, may board Broadway streetcars (buses on weekends) southbound in State Street between Monroe and Polk, or board these units northbound in Dearborn Street.

Service Intervals

Service intervals on Broadway (Route No. 36) will remain virtually unchanged, varying from two and a half to four minutes in rush hours, four to four and a half minutes in mid-day, and six minutes in the evening hours.

Owl service will operate at fifteen minute intervals.

The rather in-depth service change flier handed out by the CTA in 1955 regarding the change-over of the 36 Broadway-State streetcar route to 2 motor bus routes: 36 Broadway and 36A State Street. *Wien-Criss Archive*

For Better Service...

CLARK-WENTWORTH ROUTE REVISIONS

EFFECTIVE SEPTEMBER 8, 1957

CHICAGO TRANSIT AUTHORITY

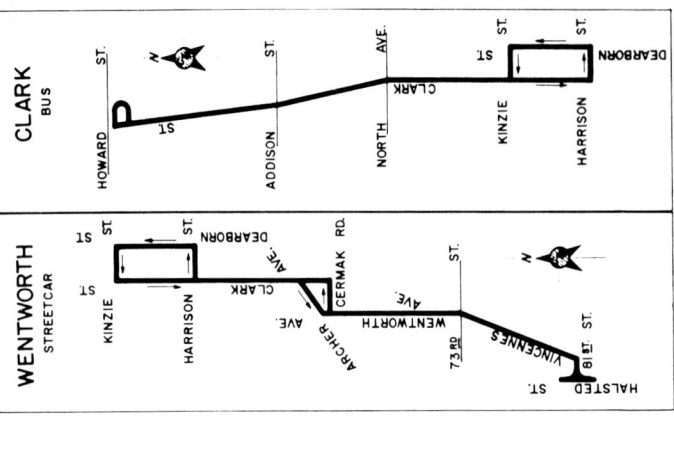

CHICAGO TRANSIT AUTHORITY'S only remaining streetcar route, Clark-Wentworth (No. 22), will be split into two parts Sunday, September 8, 1957, and buses will be substituted for streetcars between the existing north terminal at Howard Street, and a new south terminal at Harrison Street, just south of the Loop.

Seventy-one odorless propane (LP-gas) buses are assigned to this route, designated as "Clark," replacing 39 streetcars.

The south part of the former Clark-Wentworth route, now "Wentworth," is being served, Mondays through Fridays, by 48 streetcars, operating between the existing south terminal at 81st Street and Halsted Street, and Kinzie and Clark Streets, just north of the Loop. On week-ends, buses will replace the streetcars.

"Clark" Route

The routing of the "Clark" line is south in Clark Street from Howard Street to Harrison Street, east to Dearborn Street, north to Kinzie Street, west to Clark, and north to Howard.

On the Clark bus route headways during the morning and evening rush hours are reduced from two and one-half minutes to one and one-half minutes. Midday intervals remain at four minutes and evening service will continue at four to seven-minute intervals. "Owl" service operates at 30-minute intervals during the late night and early morning hours.

"Wentworth" Route

The "Wentworth" routing is east in 81st Street from Halsted Street to Vincennes Avenue, northeast to Wentworth Avenue, north to Cermak Road, east to Clark Street, north to Harrison Street, east to Dearborn Street, north to Kinzie Street, west to Clark Street, south to Archer Avenue, southwest to Wentworth, south to Vincennes, and southwest to 81st, and then west to Halsted.

On the Wentworth streetcar route headways are not changed except during the "Owl" period when 30-minute service is provided.

Advantages

Splitting of the long Clark-Wentworth route into two shorter lines provides additional service, both northbound in Dearborn Street and southbound in Clark Street for riders in the area between Kinzie Street and Harrison Street where operations of the two lines over-lap.

The shorter routes insure more regular service through closer control of operations. Service delays on one of the new, shorter routes will no longer disrupt service on the other new route, as is the case with long, through routes.

Loading Zones and Transfers

Southbound in Clark Street and northbound in Dearborn Street, between Kinzie and Harrison, Clark buses will make service stops at safety islands in the streetcar track lane. Over the rest of the route nearside curb stops will be made.

Transfers between the Clark and Wentworth routes may be made at Clark and Kinzie Streets and at Clark and Harrison Streets.

CHICAGO TRANSIT AUTHORITY

The Chicago Transit Authority issued this service change flier in 1957 to detail the splitting of the 22 Clark-Wentworth into the Clark motor bus line and the Wentworth streetcar line. The Wentworth streetcar line would see the last streetcar to run in Chicago in June of 1958. The Clark bus line retained the number 22 while the Wentworth bus line gained the number 24.

Wien-Criss Archive

Conclusion

And so it was that the year 1958 proved to be a momentous one for Walter J. McCarter. On December 31, he could look back upon the year that was ending and say to himself with great satisfaction that he had thoroughly "modernized" the CTA in his own image. As previously stated, he was totally successful in systematically dismantling the largest streetcar system in the world that he had inherited in 1947, replacing streetcars with motor and trolley buses. Simultaneously, through the conversion of PCC streetcars into PCC rapid transit cars, he succeeded in replacing all of the old wood "L" cars on the rapid transit at a cost lower than buying completely new cars. A new era in rapid transit operations was about to begin while almost a century of streetcar operation in Chicago had come to an end.

Afterword

On October 1, 1962, General Manager Walter J. McCarter completed 15 years of service to the CTA. At a special meeting of the CTA Board on October 24, 1962, the Board passed a resolution paying tribute to McCarter for his many accomplishments during his years at CTA.

It is interesting to note that one of the accomplishments for which McCarter was commended read as follows:

"…a major by-product of the modernization program, the appearance and automobile traffic capacity of many miles of Chicago streets have been greatly enhanced by the removal of streetcar rail, trolley poles, and overhead wires…"

In plain language, McCarter was commended for making the streets of Chicago more attractive for automobile traffic, the principal competitor for CTA services. Such was the mindset of many cities at the time, where the private automobile was given preferential treatment over public transit.

View of Grand Union at Madison and Clinton in September 1953 before it was preserved under layers of asphalt.
William C. Hoffman Photo, Wien-Criss Archive

COTTAGE GROVE
JUL 21
Vinc. 111th.
N
S
T
C
E
S
STAMP HERE
N.D.
SEE OTHER SIDE
TRANSFER NOT GOOD ON SURFACE DIVISION AFTER USING RAPID TRANSIT DIVISION UNLESS THE TIME IS STAMPED ON TRANSFER WHEN LEAVING RAPID TRANSIT STATION.
108074

4
DOWNTOWN
ENTER AT FRONT
57
4008
HOTE
FLORE

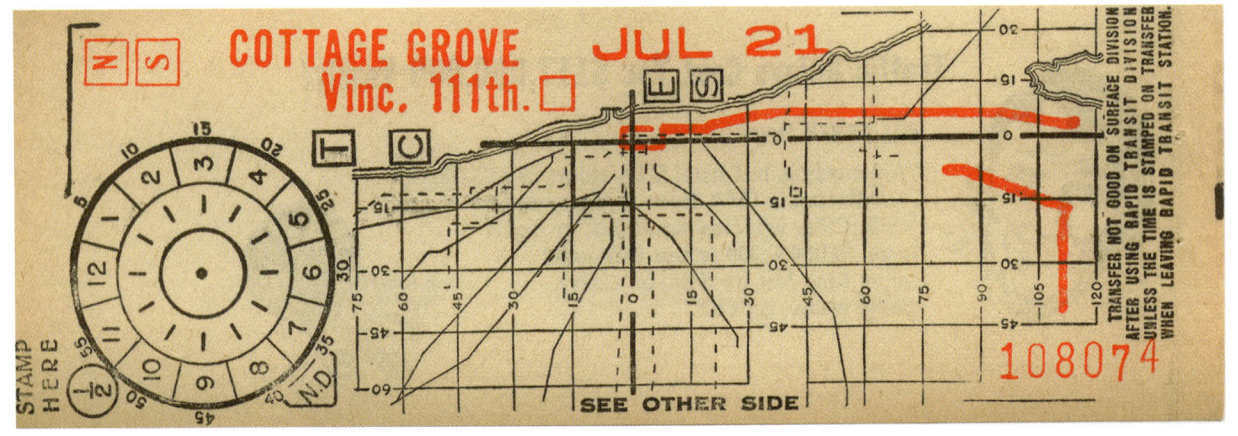

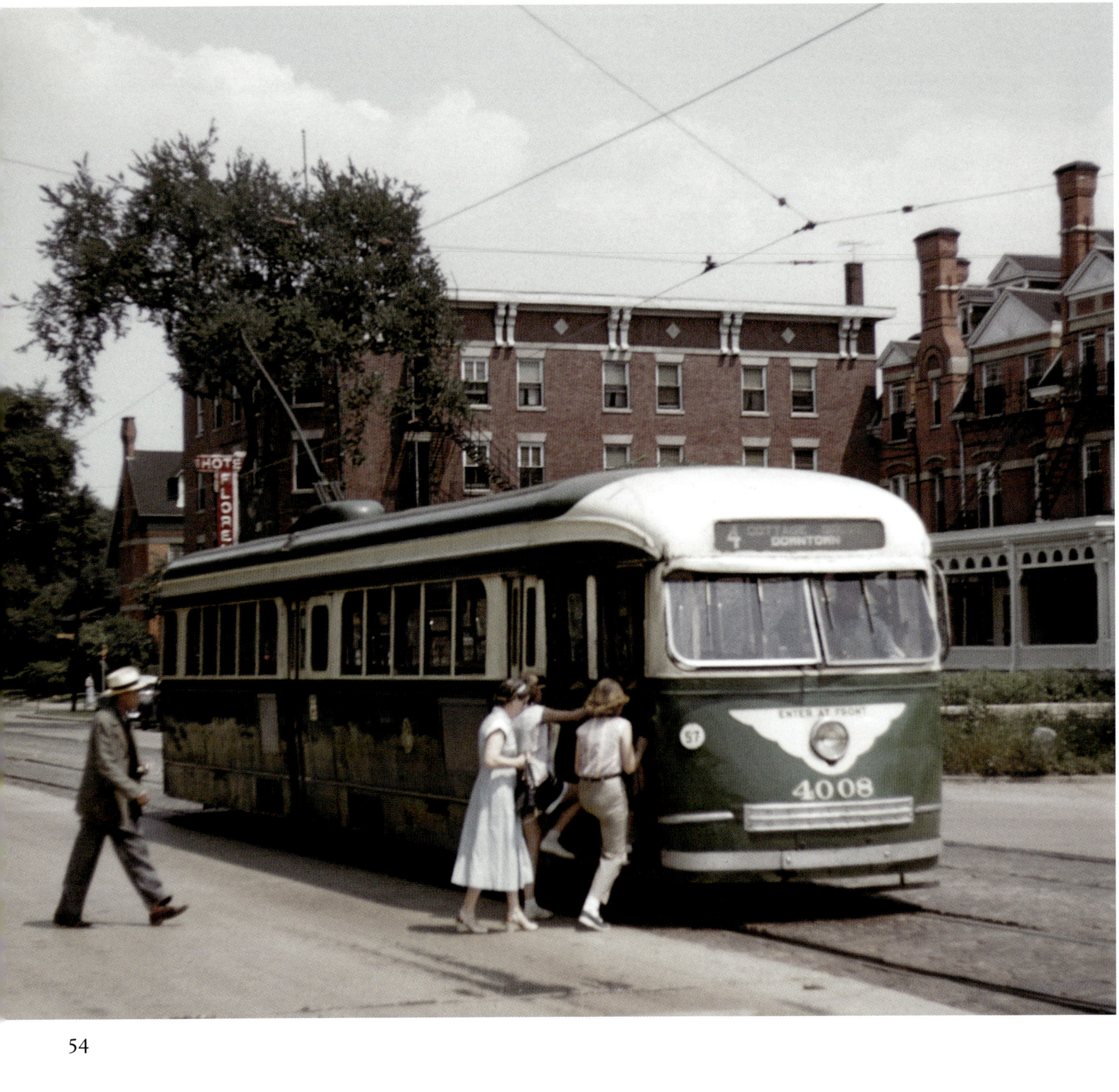

Route 4: Cottage Grove

PCC Operations History

May 11, 1952
Began operation of one-man cars using converted prewar and postwar PCCs.

June, 29, 1952
Rerouted cars via Wabash to loop at Grand and State.

June 18, 1955
PCC cars replaced by buses.

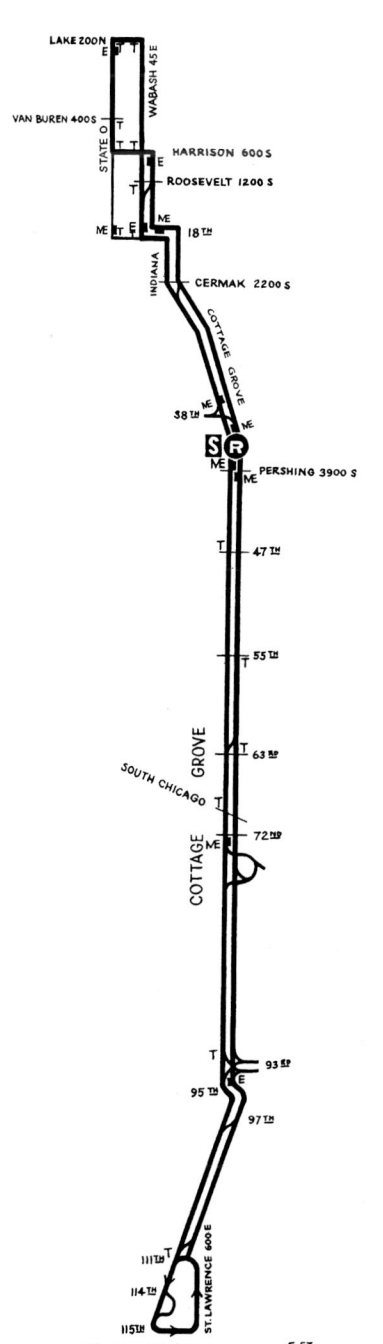

Car 7027 turning from Grand onto State, June 1952.
George Krambles Photo/Krambles-Peterson Archive

Car 4010 on State Street near Wacker Drive, May 1952.
Bernard L. Stone, Photo/John Bromley Collection

Car 4038 at Wabash and Wacker, February 1953.
Truman D. Hefner Photo

Car 4056 at State and Wacker, May 1952.
Bernard L. Stone Photo/John Bromley Collection

Car 4023 turns east onto Lake off of State in this August 1953 view.
Truman D. Hefner Photo

Night on State Street between the Chicago and State-Lake Theaters, April 1954.
William C. Hoffman Photo/Wien-Criss Archive

Car 4049 heading south at State and Lake in July 1952, getting ready to pass under the Lake Street "L." The famed Shangri-La restaurant, open from 1944 to 1968, is seen in the background.
Krambles-Peterson Archive

Car 4017 at State and Randolph, March 1955
Bernard L. Stone Photo/Krambles-Peterson Archive

Car 7005 at Wabash and Lake, May 1955.
Robert W. Gibson Photo/Electric Railway Historical Society Collection

Car 7011 near State and Jackson, December 1954.
Raymond DeGroote Photo

Car 4008 near Wabash and Jackson, in front of Central Camera, where many Chicago railfans had their film developed, May 1955.
Robert W. Gibson Photo/Electric Railway Historical Society Collection

Car 4033 westbound on Harrison at State, June 1955.
Bernard A. Rossbach Photo

Car 4054 near Wabash and Harrison, August 1954.
William C. Hoffman Photo/Wien-Criss Archive

Car 4034 at Wabash and Harrison, March 1955.
William C. Hoffman, photo/Wien-Criss Archive

Car 4044 at State and Harrison, 1954, the present site of University Center, where CERA programs are held.
Robert W. Gibson Photo/Electric Railway Historical Society Collection

Car 4037 at Wabash and 15th in March 1954.
Eugene Van Dusen Photo/Strahorn Library, Illinois Railway Museum

63

Car 4042 on Wabash at Balbo, 1954.
Robert W. Gibson Photo/Electric Railway Historical Society Collection

Car 7058 heads south on Indiana at Cermak, October 1952.
William C. Hoffman Photo/Wien-Criss Archive

Car 4003 on Cermak at Indiana, May 1954.
Bernard A. Rossbach Photo

Car 7010 on Cottage Grove at Cermak, October 1952.
William C. Hoffman Photo/Wien-Criss Archive

Car 7021 on Cottage Grove at 24th in 1955.
R. Burns Photo/Krambles-Peterson Archive

Car 4049 on Cottage Grove near 33rd in January 1955, showing the beginnings of "urban renewal."
Robert W. Gibson Photo/Electric Railway Historical Society Collection

Car 7041 on Cottage Grove at 34th, March 1953.
Robert W. Gibson Photo/John Bromley Collection

Car 4029 on Cottage Grove near 34th, January 1954.
Truman D. Hefner Photo

Car 4049 on Cottage Grove near 36th, with the Lake Meadows high-rises in the background in 1954.
Robert V. Mehlenbeck Photo/Krambles-Peterson Archive

Car 4055 on Cottage Grove at 37th in 1954.
Robert W. Gibson Photo/Electric Railway Historical Society Collection

Car 4016 on 38th at Cottage Grove Station (carbarn). This was a 1936 PCC that had been modified for one-man operation. Note that there is only one center door and three doors in front. The rear door was removed. This was the only car with this door arrangement (1952).
Bernard L. Stone Photo/John Bromley Collection

Car 4055 on Cottage Grove at 38th, August 1953.
Bernard A. Rossbach Photo

The line-up at the Cottage Grove Station at 38th and Cottage Grove, September 1954.
William C. Hoffman Photo/Wien-Criss Archive

Car 4031 on Cottage Grove at 51st, May 1953.
William C. Janssen Photo/Krambles-Peterson Archive

Car 4040 on Cottage Grove near 51st, on a rare short stretch of parallel overhead wire. Two Marmon trolley coaches from Route 51 are seen here in November 1955.
William C. Hoffman Photo/Wien-Criss Archive

Car 4015 on Cottage Grove at the Midway Plaisance, August 1952.
William C. Janssen Photo/Krambles-Peterson Archive

Car 4038 on Cottage Grove near 63rd, August 1954. The famous Trianon Ballroom, at 6201 S. Cottage Grove, can be seen in the background. It opened in 1922 and closed around the time this picture was taken. The building was demolished in 1967.
William C. Hoffman Photo/Wien-Criss Archive

Car 4017 at Cottage Grove and 63rd, June 1955. The Tivoli Theater, seen in the background, was the first of the "big three" movie palaces built by Balaban & Katz. It opened in 1921 and closed in 1963, and was demolished shortly thereafter.
George Krambles Photo/Krambles-Peterson Archive

Car 4049 on Cottage Grove, crossing under the Cottage Grove "L" station at 63rd on the Jackson Park branch, August 1954. The "L" has since been cut back to this point.
William C. Hoffman Photo/Wien-Criss Archive

Car 4039 at Cottage Grove and South Chicago, May 1955.
William C. Janssen Photo/Krambles-Peterson Archive

Car 4028 on Cottage Grove near 67th, June 1955.
Robert W. Gibson Photo/Electric Railway Historical Society Collection

Car 4035 on Cottage Grove at 70th, June 1955.
Krambles-Peterson Archive

Car 4015 at the off-street loop at Cottage Grove and 72nd, August 1953.
Bernard A. Rossbach Photo

Car 4037 turning onto Cottage Grove from the off-street loop at 72nd, August 1953.
Bernard A. Rossbach Photo

Car 7026 in the off-street loop at Cottage Grove and 72nd, May 1955.
William C. Janssen Photo/Krambles-Peterson Archive

Car 7026 turning onto Cottage Grove from an off-street loop at 72nd, May 1955.
William C. Janssen Photo/Krambles-Peterson Archive

Car 4028 passes 4002 at Cottage Grove and 72nd, August 1953.
Bernard A. Rossbach Photo

Car 4032 on Cottage Grove at 72nd, May 1955.
William C. Janssen Photo/Krambles-Peterson Archive

Car 7008 on Cottage Grove at 79th, June 1952.
CERA Archives

Car 4015 on Cottage Grove at 87th, March 1954.
George Krambles Photo/Krambles-Peterson Archive

Car 4037 on Cottage Grove near 85th, May 1955.
Truman D. Hefner Photo

Car 4037 on Cottage Grove near 85th, May 1955, with a good view of some typical Chicago-style postwar brick apartment buildings.
William C. Janssen Photo/Krambles-Peterson Archive

Car 4019 on Cottage Grove at 88th, June 1955.
Krambles-Peterson Archive

Car 4040 on Cottage Grove at 90th, March 1954.
William C. Janssen Photo/Krambles-Peterson Archive

Car 4020 on Cottage Grove at 93rd, June 1954.
Truman D. Hefner Photo

Car 4056 on Cottage Grove at 94th, taken from the Illinois Central embankment, November 1954.
James J. Buckley Photo/CERA Archives

Car 4023 crossing under the Illinois Central embankment at Cottage Grove and 95th, March 1954.
William C. Janssen Photo/Krambles-Peterson Archive

Car 4039 on Cottage Grove private right-of-way near 96th, 1953.
Robert V. Mehlenbeck Photo/Krambles-Peterson Archive

Car 4042 on private right-of-way at Cottage Grove and 96th, May 1955.
William C. Janssen Photo/Krambles-Peterson Archive

Car 4013 on private right-of-way at Cottage Grove near 99th, with the 95th Street shops of the Illinois Central Electric Suburban Division in the background, in February 1955.
William C. Janssen Photo/Krambles-Peterson Archive

Car 7022 on private right-of-way at Cottage Grove and 98th, May 1955. The Jay's Potato Chips factory is at left.
William C. Janssen Photo/Krambles-Peterson Archive

Car 4013 on private right-of-way near Cottage Grove and 97th, February 1955.
William C. Janssen Photo/Krambles-Peterson Archive

Streetcar tracks are already being dismantled at Cottage Grove near 97th, only a few days after the end of service, June 1955.
William C. Hoffman Photo/Wien-Criss Archive

Car 4054 on private right-of-way at Cottage Grove and 100th, July 1953.
Robert W. Gibson Photo/John Bromley Collection

Car 4006 northbound on private right-of-way near Cottage Grove and 103rd, February 1955.
William C. Janssen Photo/Krambles-Peterson Archive

Car 4026 southbound on private right-of-way near Cottage Grove and 103rd in 1955.
William C. Janssen Photo/Krambles-Peterson Archive

Car 4053 on private right-of-way near Cottage Grove and 103rd, February 1955.
William C. Janssen Photo/Krambles-Peterson Archive

Car 7044 passes Car 4015 on private right-of-way near Cottage Grove and 103rd, March 1954.
George Krambles Photo/Krambles-Peterson Archive

Car 4008 picks up passengers, northbound on 111th at Cottage Grove, on the last day of streetcar service, June 18, 1955. The famous Hotel Florence in the historic Pullman neighborhood is in the background.
George Krambles Photo/Krambles-Peterson Archive

Car 4009 on Cottage Grove at 111th, June 1954.
Bernard A. Rossbach Photo

Car 4015 on 111th at Cottage Grove, near the Illinois Central embankment and station, March 1954.
George Krambles Photo/Krambles-Peterson Archive

Car 4015 on 111th at Forrestville, March 1955.
Krambles-Peterson Archive

Car 4018 on private right-of-way at Cottage Grove and 112th, February 1955.
William C. Janssen Photo/Krambles-Peterson Archive

Car 4008 on private right-of-way at Cottage Grove and 112th, November 1954.
Bernard A. Rossbach Photo

Car 7020 on St. Lawrence and 111th, May 1955.
Robert W. Gibson Photo/Electric Railway Historical Society Collection

Car 4012 on St. Lawrence and 112th in a pleasant view from September 1953.
Bernard A. Rossbach Photo

Car 4039 on private right-of-way at Cottage Grove and 112th, June 1954.
Bernard A. Rossbach Photo

Car 7064 on private right-of-way at Cottage Grove and 112th, November 1952, with the Florence Hotel in the background.
William C. Janssen Photo/Krambles-Peterson Archive

Car 4015 on St. Lawrence at 114th, March 1954, with a good view of the brick row houses in the historic Pullman neighborhood.
William C. Janssen Photo/Krambles-Peterson Archive

Car 4006 turning from 115th to St. Lawrence, February 1955.
William C. Janssen Photo/Krambles-Peterson Archive

Four prewar PCCs, with car 4036 at the rear, are laying over at the end of the line at Cottage Grove and 115th, 1952.
Robert V. Mehlenbeck Photo/Krambles-Peterson Archive

Car 4049 on 115th at St. Lawrence, June 1955.
John R. Williams Photo/Krambles-Peterson Archive

Car 4049, signed for route 38 and with three cars parked behind, prepares to head north from the end of the line at Cottage Grove and 115th, June 1955. CTA had cars signed for route 38 (which was actually Indiana Avenue, a stub-end line where no PCCs ever ran) because there was no appropriate sign curtain available that read Grand and State. So this was the next best thing.
Robert V. Mehlenbeck Photo/Krambles-Peterson Archive

Car 7011, signed for route 38, begins its trip north by turning from Cottage Grove onto 115th, 1952. *William C. Janssen Photo/Krambles-Peterson Archive*

Car 7030 begins its northbound run, turning from Cottage Grove to 115th, 1954.
Robert W. Gibson Photo/Electric Railway Historical Society Collection

HALSTED Ext. D. T. MAR 25
S Vinc.-111th
STAMP HERE
N.D.
SEE OTHER SIDE
654373
TRANSFER NOT GOOD ON SURFACE DIVISION AFTER USING RAPID TRANSIT DIVISION UNLESS THE TIME IS STAMPED ON TRANSFER WHEN LEAVING RAPID TRANSIT STATION.

8 HALSTED-79TH
7051

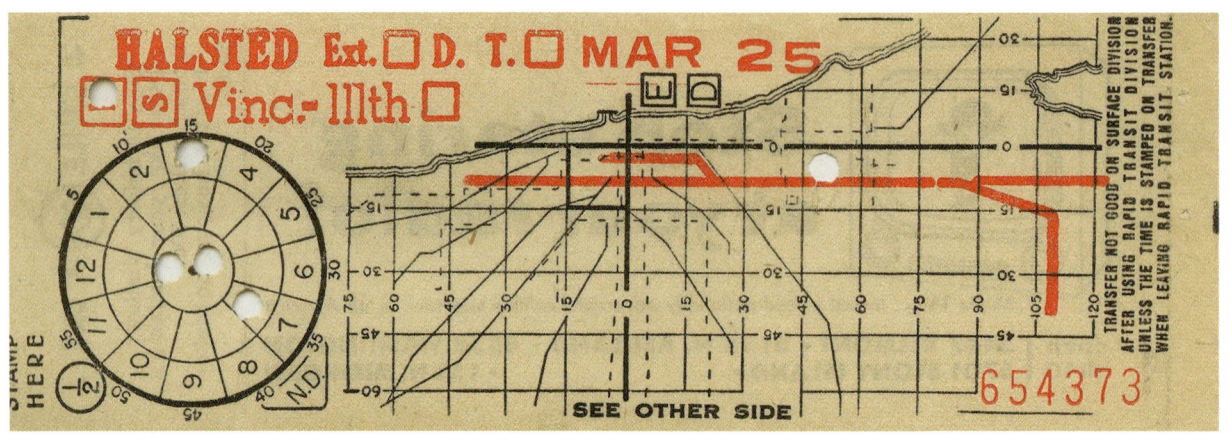

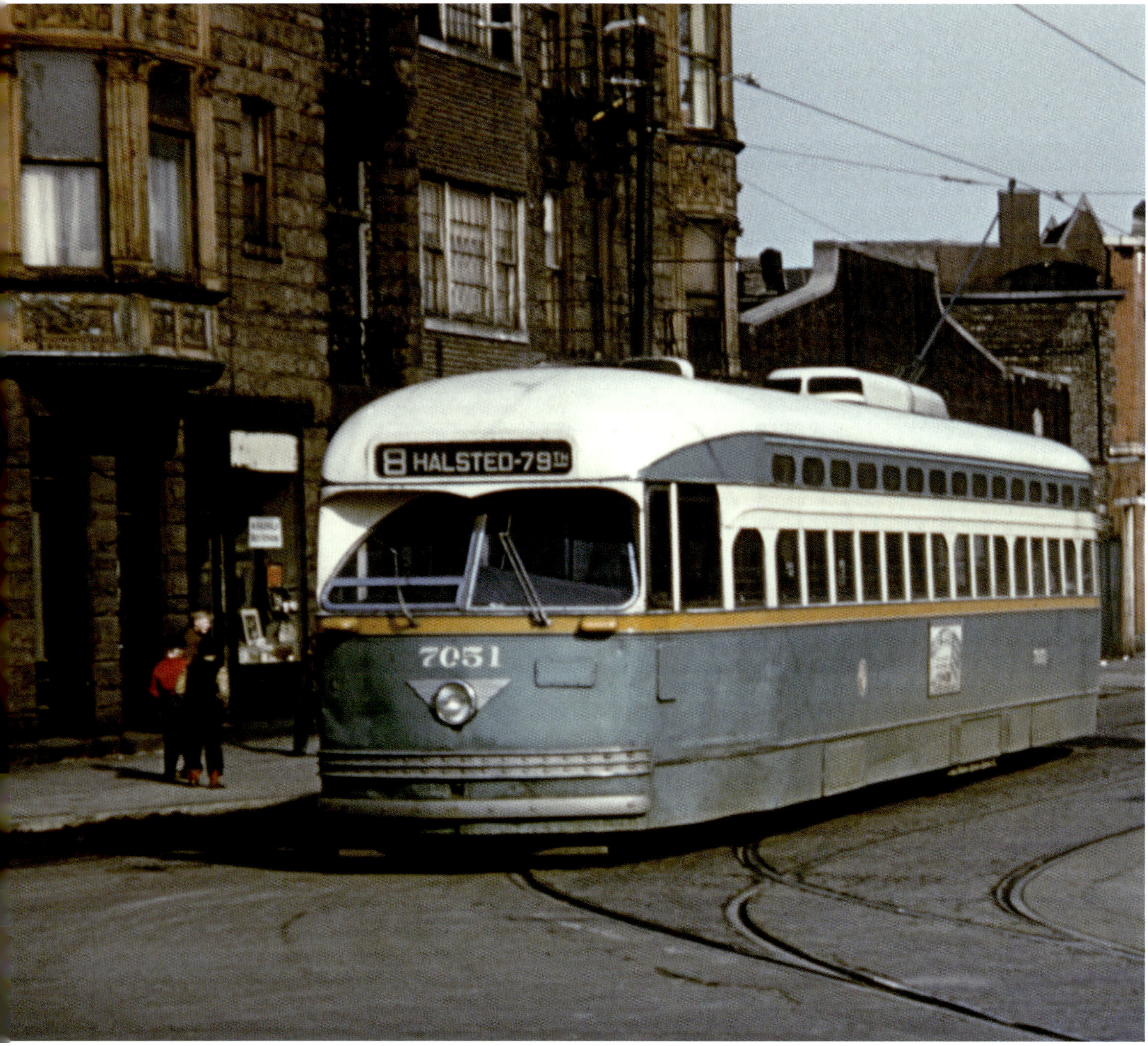

Route 8: Halsted

PCC Operations History

December 4, 1949
PCCs introduced to route; mixed operation with standard red cars. Service cut back to loop at 79th and Halsted.

July 1950
Service operated completely by PCCs.

November 24, 1951
Buses substituted for streetcars on weekends.

June 1953
Begin gradual replacement of PCC cars with standard red cars. Route operated exclusively by standard streetcars by end of 1953.

May 29, 1954
Streetcars replaced by buses.

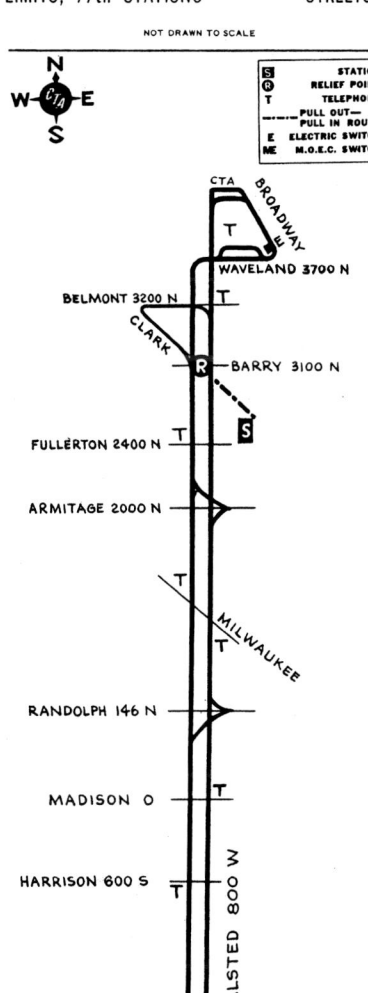

Car 7051 at the Halsted-Waveland loop, February 1954.
Truman D. Hefner Photo

Car 7051 at Halsted and Waveland, February 1954.
Truman D. Hefner Photo

Car 7050 on Halsted, Lincoln, and Fullerton, 1952.
Michael Raia Collection

Car 4151 on Halsted at Armitage, 1952.
Michael Raia Collection

Car 7151 on Halsted at Division, near the Ogden overpass (which has since been torn down), 1952. This is near the site of the former Cabrini-Green housing project.
Michael Raia Collection

Car 4127 on Halsted at Division, passing under the old Ogden overpass, December 1953.
Bernard A. Rossbach Photo

Car 7239 on Chicago Avenue east of Halsted, during a reroute in December 1953. The architecturally significant Montgomery Wards Company Complex, a Chicago landmark since converted to upscale condos, is in the background. The car is operating on shared wire with the 66 trolley bus, an uncommon practice in Chicago.
Bernard A. Rossbach Photo

Car 7031 on Halsted at Grand and Milwaukee, 1954, previously the site of a Grand Union. The Route 42 destination sign is incorrect.
Truman D. Hefner Photo

Car 4149 on Halsted shoo-fly, passes under the old Met "L" during construction of the Congress Expressway, September 1950.
Henry Stange Jr. Photo/Krambles-Peterson Archive

Car 4366 on Halsted shoo-fly during construction of the Congress Expressway, September 1950. Notice Klein's Sporting Goods in the background.
Henry Stange Jr. Photo/Krambles-Peterson Archive

Car 4223 on Halsted shoo-fly, with the old Met "L" in the background, during bridge construction for the Congress Expressway, September 1950.
Henry Stange Jr. Photo/Krambles-Peterson Archive

Car 4206 on Halsted shoo-fly during construction of the Congress Expressway, October 1950.
William C. Hoffman Photo/Wien-Criss Archive

Car 4342 on Halsted shoo-fly, going around the new bridge over the Congress Expressway, then under construction, June 1951.
Robert W. Gibson Photo/CERA Archives

Car 4258 on Halsted shoo-fly during construction of the Congress Expressway, May 1952. The new tracks in the foreground lead up to the bridge over the highway. The bridges were built first, before the rest of the expressway was dug out.
CERA Archives

Car 4265 on Halsted shoo-fly, during construction of the Congress Expressway, June 1952. Excavation is underway. This section of highway opened in 1955.
Bernard L. Stone Photo/Krambles-Peterson Archive

Car 4290 onHalsted shoo-fly during construction of the Congress (now Eisenhower) Expressway, June 1952. This shot was taken from the old Met "L", which was relocated into the highway median in 1958.
Bernard L. Stone Photo/Krambles-Peterson Archive

Car 7184 on Halsted and Congress, August 1953. The new highway bridge has been finished.
Bernard A. Rossbach Photo

Car 4283 is northbound on Halsted at Archer, 1952, with a Santa Fe passenger train in view at rear.
Michael Raia Collection

Car 4370 on Halsted at 42nd in July 1952, when the Democratic Convention was being held at the International Amphitheatre (right side of photo), built in 1934 and demolished in 1999. Illinois Governor Adlai E. Stevenson II, was nominated for President, losing to Gen. Dwight D. Eisenhower, who had become the Republican standard bearer in the same hall only a few weeks earlier.
Robert W. Gibson Photo/Electric Railway Historical Society Collection

Car 7173 is illuminated by neon in this night shot taken from the Englewood "L" in April 1954. From the lights, you can sense the vibrancy and activity of this then-bustling shopping area, so typical of Chicago in the 1950s. Such scenes have long since given way to urban decay, strip malls, and shopping centers with large parking lots. *William C. Hoffman Photo/Wien-Criss Archive*

Car 4307 on 63rd Place, getting ready to turn north onto Halsted, in August 1953, with the Englewood "L" at left. *Truman D. Hefner Photo*

Car 4132 is on Halsted near 75th, having just passed under a railroad overpass. Note the now long-abandoned Wabash passenger train station at left. This service was taken over by Norfolk and Western in 1964. *Michael Raia Collection*

Car 4068, getting ready to pull into the south terminal, near 79th and Emerald in February 1954.
Bernard A. Rossbach Photo

Car 4154 at the Halsted-79th loop in September 1950. Note the supervisor's shanty at right.
John E. Koschwanez Photo/John Bromley Collection

Car 7045 at the 79th-Halsted terminal in February 1954.
Bernard A. Rossbach Photo

MADISON
Fifth
HARRISON
Adams
OCT 10
STAMP HERE
N.D
282570
TRANSFER NOT GOOD ON SURFACE DIVISIO
AFTER USING RAPID TRANSIT DIVISIO
UNLESS THE TIME IS STAMPED ON TRANSFE
WHEN LEAVING RAPID TRANSIT STATIO

20 MADISON-DOWNTOWN
4113
36
ENTER AT REAR
ONE MAN OPERATION

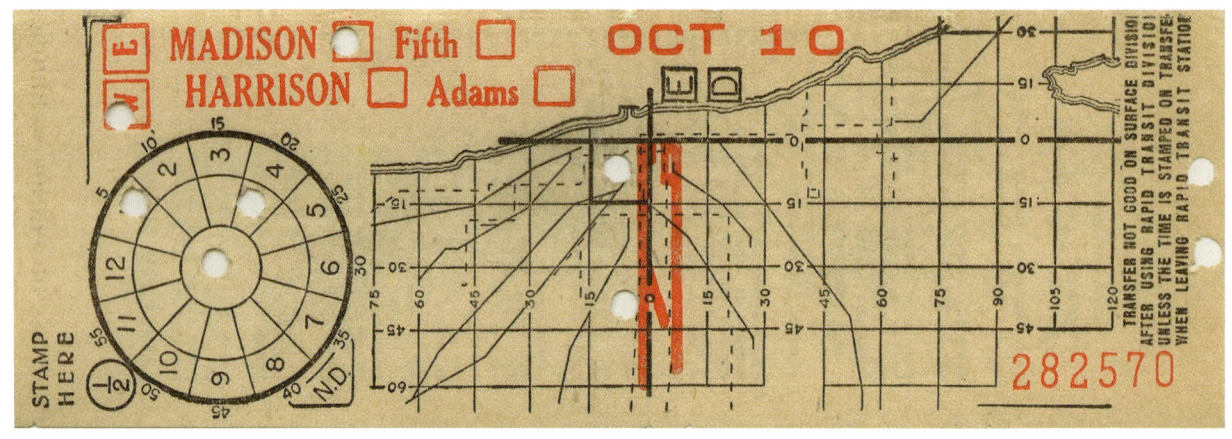

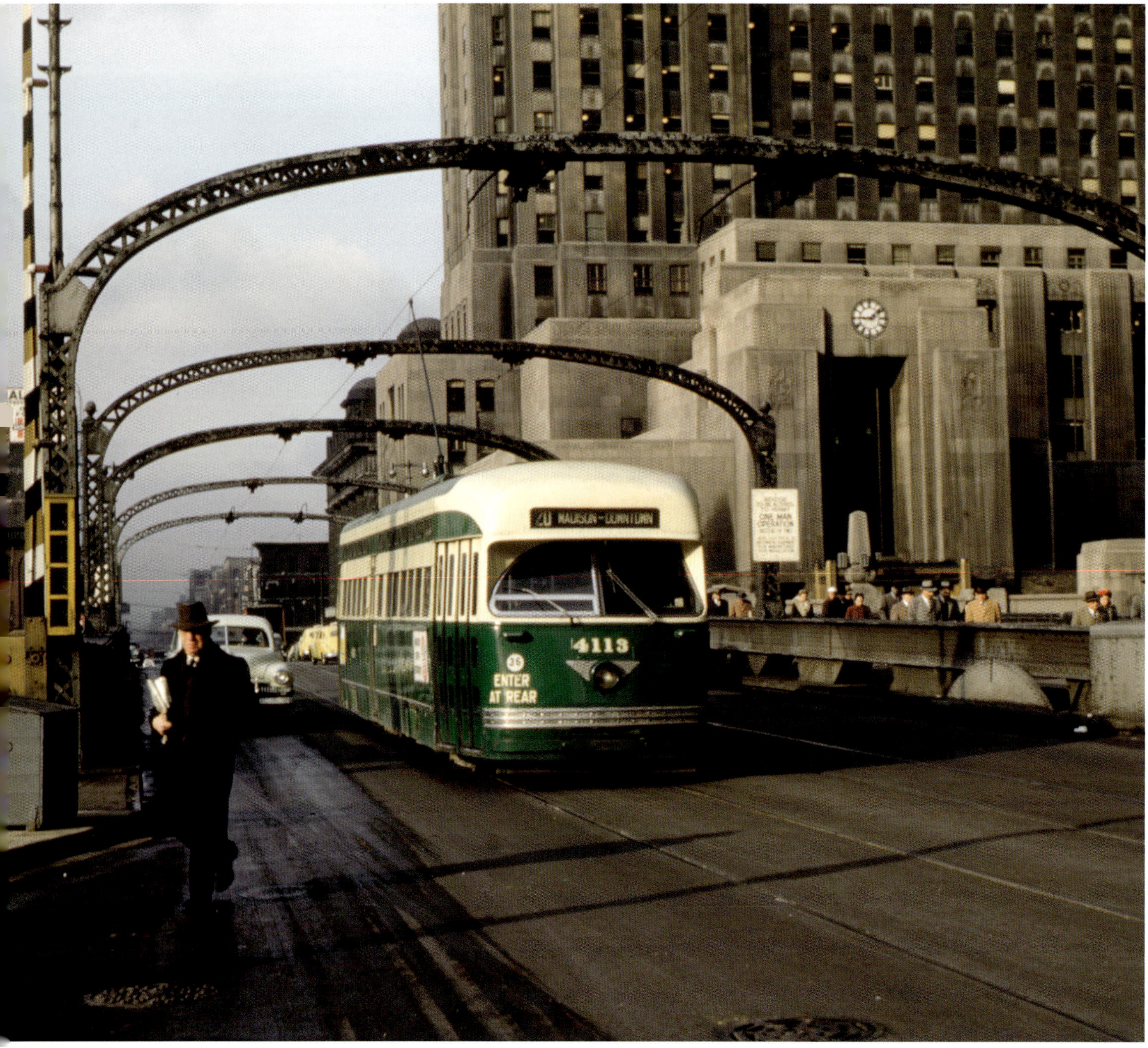

Route 20: Madison – Madison/Fifth

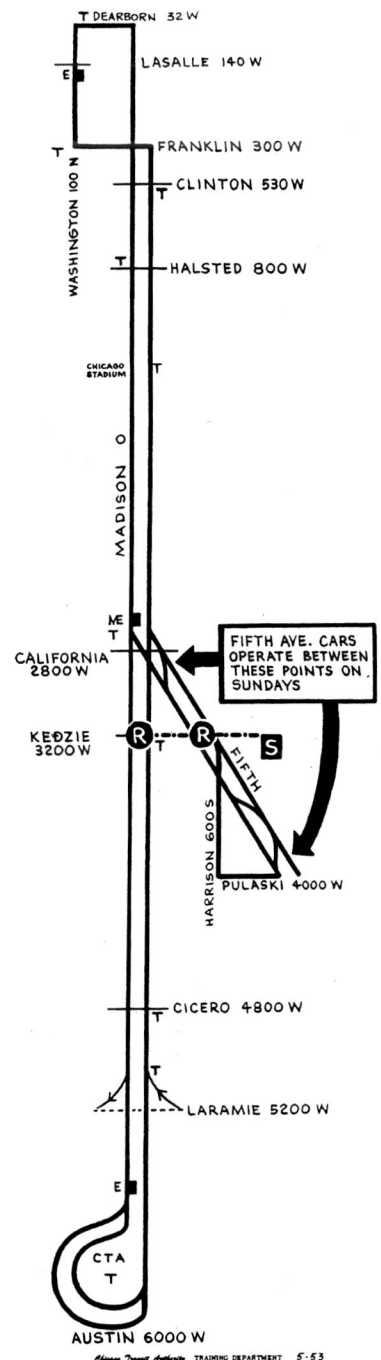

PCC Operations History

September 13, 1936
PCC operation in Chicago commences.

February 1937
All 83 new PCC cars in service. Sedans are used to augment weekday service on both routes.

Early 1948
Introduction of new postwar PCCs to gradually replace all prewar PCC cars. Conversion to new PCC operation completed by June 1948.

October 17, 1949
Begin operation of 10-cent AM and PM shuttle with the prewar PCCs.

July 31, 1951
Both shuttles discontinued without replacement.

November 10, 1951
Streetcars rerouted via Madison to loop via Desplaines, Washington (via the streetcar tunnel), and Dearborn.

May 11, 1952
Buses substituted for streetcars on weekends on main Madison Street route.

May 17, 1952
Buses substituted for streetcars on Saturdays on Madison-Fifth.

December 12, 1953
Buses replace PCC cars on Madison. Standard red streetcars replace PCCs on Madison-Fifth and operated as shuttles.

Car 4009, wearing "tiger stripes," is at the Madison-Austin loop in June 1946.
CERA Archives

Car 4046 on the Madison-Austin off-street loop in July 1938.
Bernard L. Stone Photo/John Bromley Collection

Car 4074 basks in sunlight in this June 1950 view at the Madison-Austin loop.
Krambles-Peterson Archive

Cars 4143 and 4098 on the off-street Madison-Austin loop in July 1950. The ads on the sides of the cars promote the Ringling Brothers Barnum & Bailey Circus, then appearing at Soldier Field.
Krambles-Peterson Archive

Cars 4100 and 4112 lay over at the Madison-Austin loop in March 1949.
George Krambles Photo/Krambles-Peterson Archive

Car 4112 on the Madison-Austin loop in March 1949.
George Krambles Photo/Krambles-Peterson Archive

Car 4115 pulling out onto Madison from the Austin loop in August 1948, in this view taken from a nearby building. Note that the old track connection with the Chicago and West Towns Railways has already been bricked over. *CERA Archives*

Car 4143 at the Madison-Austin loop in July 1950. *George Krambles Photo/Krambles-Peterson Archive*

Car 4090 on Madison, somewhere west of Cicero Avenue, in July 1950.
Robert W. Gibson Photo/Electric Railway Historical Society Collection

PCCs 4123 and 4129 rooming with red car 1693 in this circa 1949 view at Kedzie Station.
Krambles-Peterson Archive

Cars 4033 and 4002 in original livery at Kedzie Station in October 1938.
Bernard L. Stone Photo/John Bromley Collection

Car 7003, newly delivered, at Kedzie Station in November 1936.
John Bromley Collection

Car 4010 on Madison at Hamlin in January 1937. The landmark building at the corner, once a hotel, is now called the Madison Apartments.
John Bromley Collection

Car 4088 on Madison near Garfield Park in June 1950.
CERA Archives

Car 4079, on the Madison-Fifth branch line, is on Fifth Avenue at Francisco in October 1948.
George Krambles Photo/Krambles-Peterson Archive

Car 4105 on Fifth Avenue approaching Pulaski, as seen from the Garfield Park Pulaski "L" station in January 1951. *CERA Archives*

Car 4021, the only prewar PCC preserved, heads east at Harrison and Fifth in 1945. *CERA Archives*

Car 4102, signed for Madison-Fifth, is on Fifth Avenue at Harrison in June 1950. This was a branch line from the main Madison route and ran to the southwest from this point to Pulaski Road. Madison-Fifth service was discontinued in 1953, when Fifth was bisected by the construction of the Congress Expressway. (No overpass was ever built.) Note that this PCC does not have a CTA or CSL logo on the side.
CERA Archives

Car 4070 on Madison at Hermitage, after passing under the Madison stop on the old Northwest branch of the Met "L". By the time this picture was taken in October 1953, service at this station had been discontinued for nearly three years, with the opening of the Milwaukee-Dearborn subway in February 1951. Douglas Park trains were routed this way from 1954-1958, during construction of the Congress Expressway, and this is the current routing of today's Pink Line, but the station was never reactivated, and the station house was torn down in the late 1990s.
Bernard L. Stone Photo/John Bromley Collection

Car 4051, wearing "tiger stripes" to alert motorists that PCCs were wider than older streetcars, is on Madison near Hermitage in August 1946.
Bernard L. Stone Photo/John Bromley Collection

Car 4023 turning from Monroe onto Clinton in March 1943.
Strahorn Library, Illinois Railway Museum

Car 4026, signed for the Madison-Fifth branch line, has just made the turn from Monroe onto Clinton in March 1943.
Strahorn Library, Illinois Railway Museum

Car 4149, still wearing a CSL logo, is at Madison and Canal in August 1948, having just passed the old Chicago & North Western station, which was largely demolished in 1984 and replaced with today's Ogilvie Transportation Center. Note the 1948 Chrysler at left, and the 1947 Cadillac at right.
CERA Archives

Car 4048 on Madison at Canal in October 1950, passing by the old Chicago Daily News Building.
William C. Hoffman Photo/Wien-Criss Archive

Car 4064 on Madison near Canal in November 1953. The old Chicago Daily News Building is at right, with the Chicago & North Western station behind that.
William C. Hoffman Photo/Wien-Criss Archive

Car 4113 on the Madison Street bascule bridge over the Chicago River in November 1953. The old Chicago Daily News Building is in the background.
William C. Hoffman Photo/Wien-Criss Archive

Car 4095 is eastbound on Madison at Wacker in 1953.
William C. Janssen Photo/Krambles-Peterson Archive

Car 4095 is eastbound on Madison at Wacker, passing the landmark Civic Opera House at right, in 1953.
William C. Janssen Photo/Krambles-Peterson Archive

Car 4131 passes car 570 at Madison and Wacker on a shoo-fly in June 1952, during construction of the Wacker Drive extension.
CERA Archives

Car 4073 on Madison at Franklin in 1952, entering a Grand Union.
J. Pilling Jr. Photo/Michael Raia Collection

Car 4112 turning from Madison onto Franklin in 1953.
William C. Janssen Photo/Krambles-Peterson Archive

Car 4117 and its follower are turning from Madison onto Franklin on December 11, 1953, the last day of streetcar service on Route 20. Newspaper trucks in the background advertise the old *Chicago American*.
Bernard A. Rossbach Photo

Car 4132 is eastbound, turning from Franklin to Madison in 1950.
Bernard L. Stone Photo/Krambles-Peterson Archive

Car 4066 eastbound on Madison near Franklin in 1953, passing DeMet's Candies at right.
CERA Archives

CLARK WENTWORTH NOV 9
Broadway-State
STAMP HERE
SEE OTHER SIDE
321883
TRANSFER NOT GOOD ON SURFACE DIVISION AFTER USING RAPID TRANSIT DIVISION UNLESS THE TIME IS STAMPED ON TRANSFER

WRIGLEY FIELD
HOME OF
CHICAGO CUBS
TICKETS NOW ALL GAMES
NEW YORK JULY 23 24 25
7222

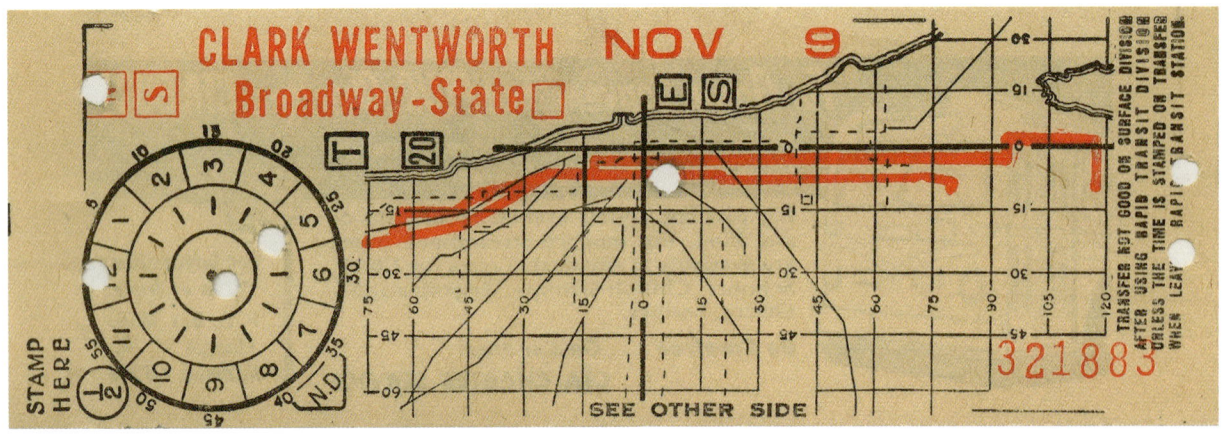

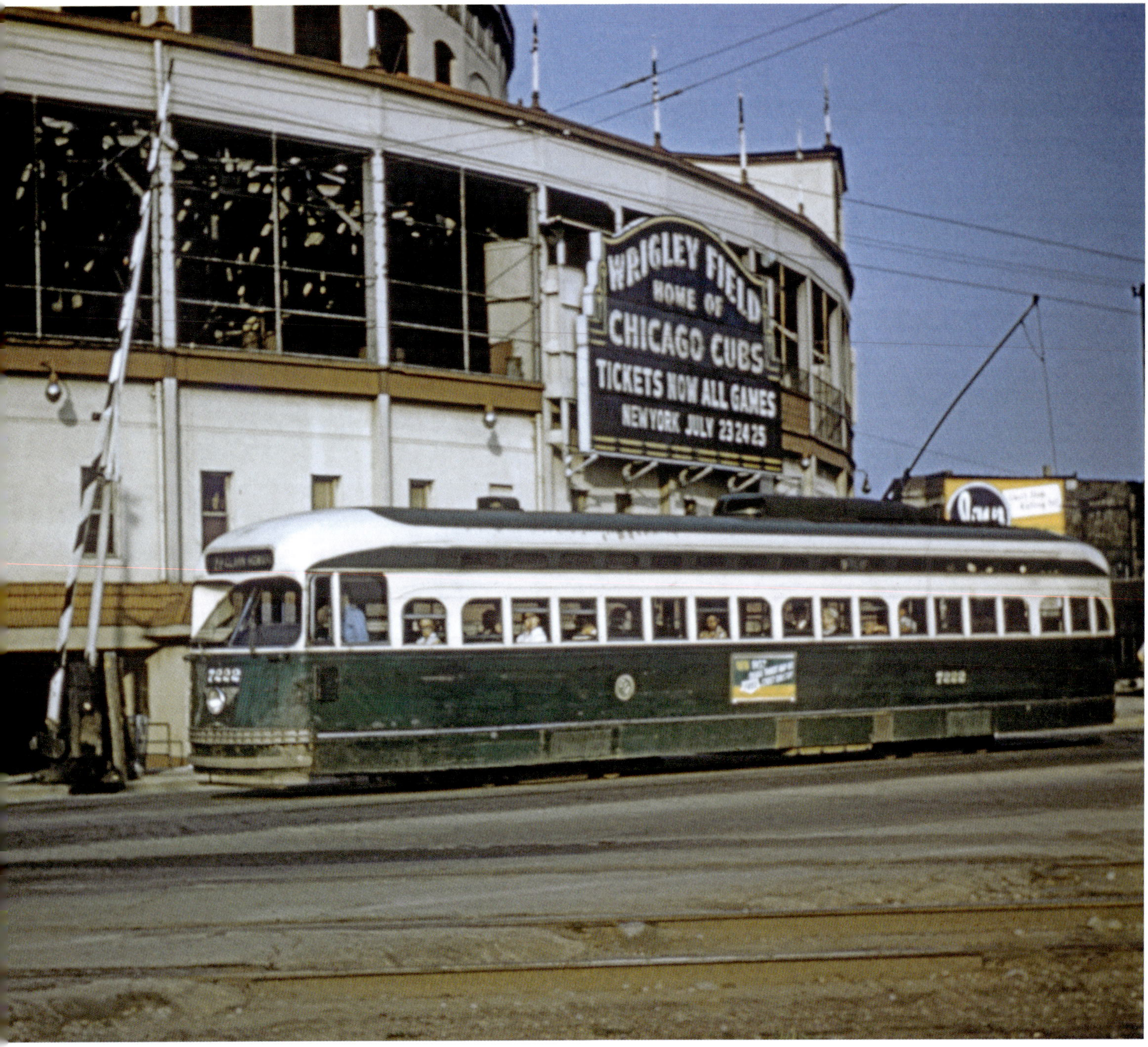

Route 22: Clark/Wentworth

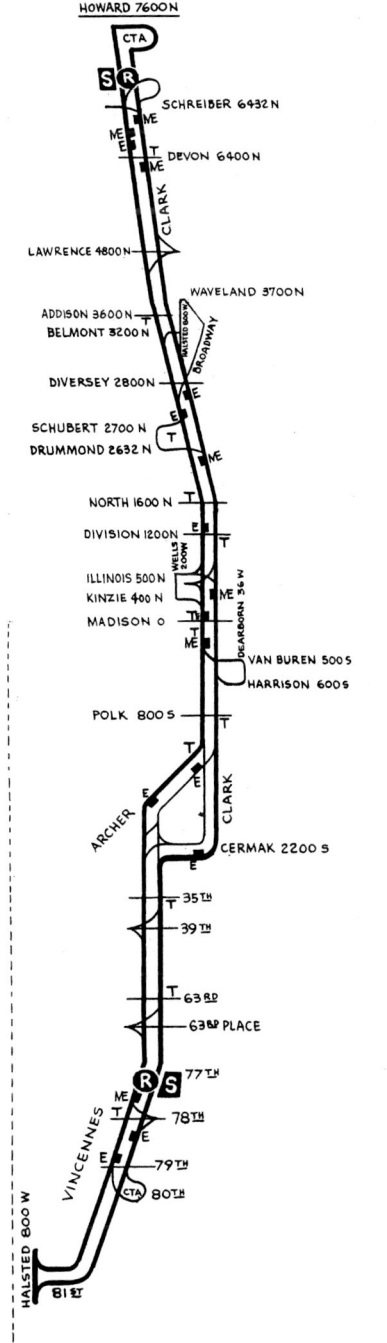

PCC Operations History

October 30, 1946
PCCs gradually introduced into service under Chicago Surface Lines management. All service was by PCCs beginning in 1947.

November 15, 1953
PCCs rerouted in Loop via Clark, Harrison, Dearborn, Kinzie, and Clark due to new one-way streets.

September 5, 1954
Buses substituted for PCCs on weekends.

September 7, 1957
PCCs replaced by buses on Clark section (Clark-Kinzie to Clark-Howard). Wentworth section becomes last streetcar line in Chicago.

June 21, 1958
Last streetcar in Chicago finished its run at 6:00 a.m.

Car 4253 pulling out of the Clark-Howard Loop onto Clark in July 1953.
Thomas H. Desnoyers Photo/Krambles-Peterson Archive

Car 4404 pulling out of the Clark-Howard Loop onto Clark in September 1957.
Charles L. Tauscher Photo/Wien-Criss Archive

Car 7070 laying over in the Clark-Howard Loop in July 1954.
George Krambles Photo/Krambles-Peterson Archive

Car 7144 laying over in the Clark-Howard Loop in September 1957 picking up passengers.
Kenneth J. Spengler Photo

Car 7168 ready to enter Clark-Howard Loop in July 1954.
William C. Janssen Photo/Krambles-Peterson Archive

Car 7168 preparing to enter Clark-Howard Loop in July 1954.
George Krambles Photo/Krambles-Peterson Archive

Car 7168 pulling into the Clark-Howard Loop as Car 7270 has just pulled out of the loop in July 1954.
William C. Janssen Photo/Krambles-Peterson Archive

Car 7168 pulling around the Clark-Howard Loop in July 1954.
William C. Janssen Photo/Krambles-Peterson Archive

Car 7180 laying over in Clark-Howard Loop in July 1957.
Charles L. Tauscher Photo/Wien-Criss Archive

Car 7192 entering Clark-Howard Loop in June 1957.
Robert W. Gibson Photo/Electric Railway Historical Society Collection

Car 7224 pulling into the Clark-Howard Loop as seen from standing on a billboard across the street in September 1957.
Kenneth J. Spengler Photo

Car 7224 pulling out of Clark-Howard Loop as seen from standing on a billboard across the street in September 1957.
Kenneth J. Spengler Photo

Car 7233 laying over in the Clark-Howard Loop in April 1954.
Bernard A. Rossbach Photo

Car 4393 at Clark and Birchwood in January 1957.
Robert W. Gibson Photo/Electric Railway Historical Society Collection

Car 7213 on Clark north of Rogers in June 1957.
Robert W. Gibson Photo/Electric Railway Historical Society Collection

Car 7139 at Clark and Rogers in August 1957.
William C. Janssen Photo/Krambles-Peterson Archive

Car 4375 at Clark and Chase in January 1957.
Robert W. Gibson Photo/Electric Railway Historical Society Collection

Car 4406 at Clark and Chase In August 1957.
William C. Janssen Photo/Krambles-Peterson Archive

Car 7154 at Clark and Chase in January 1957.
Robert W. Gibson Photo/Electric Railway Historical Society Collection

Car 7249 at Clark and Touhy in January 1957 with Car 7260 following.
Robert W. Gibson Photo/Electric Railway Historical Society Collection

Car 4066 at Clark and Touhy in March 1947. Note lack of Mercury Green color around standee windows.
Robert W. Gibson Photo/Electric Railway Historical Society Collection

Car 7046 in the Clark-Arthur Loop opposite the Devon Station (carbarn) in May 1954.
William C. Hoffman Photo/Wien-Criss Archive

Car 7220 in the Clark-Arthur Loop opposite the Devon Station (carbarn) in May 1954.
George Krambles Photo/Krambles-Peterson Archive

Car 7157 in the Clark-Arthur Loop looking toward the Devon Station (carbarn) in September 1957. *Kenneth J. Spengler Photo*

Car 7158 at Clark and Schreiber by Devon Station (carbarn) for a crew change in September 1957.
Kenneth J. Spengler Photo

Car 7158 in Clark-Arthur Loop as seen from the second story of the Devon Station (carbarn) across the street in August 1957.
Charles L. Tauscher Photo/Wien-Criss Archive

Car 7175 at Clark and Arthur approaching the leads from the Devon Station (carbarn) in September 1957.
Kenneth J. Spengler Photo

Car 4372 at Clark and Schreiber in August 1957 by the Devon Station (carbarn) which dated back to the Chicago Union Traction Company, a predecessor to the Chicago Railways Company.
Robert W. Gibson Photo/Electric Railway Historical Society Collection

Car 7165 at Clark and Schreiber in June 1957 by the Devon Station (carbarn).
Wien-Criss Archive

Car 7213 laying over in the handsomely landscaped Clark-Arthur Loop opposite the Devon Station in August 1957.
Charles L. Tauscher, photo/Wien-Criss Archive

Car 7143 at Schreiber and Ravenswood in September 1957 pulling into Devon Station.
Charles L. Tauscher Photo/Wien-Criss Archive

Car 7214 at Clark and Schreiber in May 1954 by Devon Station.
Raymond DeGroote Photo

Car 4402 at Clark and Devon in June 1957.
Charles L. Tauscher Photo/Wien-Criss Archive

Car 7178 at Clark and Devon in August 1957.
Robert W. Gibson Photo/Electric Railway Historical Society Collection

Car 7037 built by St. Louis Car Company and Car 4080 built by Pullman-Standard at Devon Station in June 1947. Note the differences in styling between the two car builders.
John Bromley Collection

Car 7195 at Devon Station in May 1954.
Richard C. Cerne Photo/CERA Archives

Cars 7242 and 7227 at Devon Station showing differences in liveries in July 1951.
William C. Hoffman Photo/Wien-Criss Archive

Car 7240 at Clark and Thome in January 1957.
Robert W. Gibson Photo/Electric Railway Historical Society Collection

Car 7138 at Clark and Glenlake in January 1957.
Robert W. Gibson Photo/Electric Railway Historical Society Collection

Car 7272 at Clark and Elmdale in January 1957.
Robert W. Gibson Photo/Electric Railway Historical Society Collection

Car 7179 at Clark and Elmdale in September 1957.
Robert W. Gibson Photo/Electric Railway Historical Society Collection

Car 7208 at Clark and Peterson in August 1957.
Charles L. Tauscher Photo/Wien-Criss Archive

Car 7154 at Clark and Ridge in August 1957.
Charles L. Tauscher Photo/Wien-Criss Archive

Car 7193 at Clark and Ridge in July 1957.
Charles L. Tauscher Photo/Wien-Criss Archive

Car 4406 at Clark and Ardmore in August 1957.
Kenneth J. Spengler Photo

Car 7182 at Clark and Edgewater in August 1957.
Thomas H. Desnoyers Photo/Krambles-Peterson Archive

Car 7214 at Clark and Summerdale in August 1957.
Robert W. Gibson Photo/Electric Railway Historical Society Collection

Car 7223 at Clark and Balmoral in August 1957.
Robert W. Gibson Photo/Electric Railway Historical Society Collection

Car 7212 at Clark and Carmen in August 1957.
Thomas H. Desnoyers Photo/Krambles-Peterson Archive

Car 4377 at Clark and Lawrence in August 1957.
Robert W. Gibson Photo/Electric Railway Historical Society Collection

Car 7160 at Clark and Lawrence passing the Rainbo Arena in September 1957, the year it was converted to an ice rink. The Rainbo served as a practice rink for the Chicago Black Hawks (as the name was spelled then) for many years.
Charles L. Tauscher Photo/Wien-Criss Archive

Car 7198 at Clark and Pensacola in August 1957.
Thomas H. Desnoyers Photo/Krambles-Peterson Archive

Car 7139 at Clark and Berteau in August 1957.
Thomas H. Desnoyers Photo/Krambles-Peterson Archive

Car 4399 at Clark north of Irving Park in August 1957.
Robert W. Gibson Photo/Electric Railway Historical Society Collection

Car 7141 on Clark near Southport in August 1957.
Robert W. Gibson Photo/Electric Railway Historical Society Collection

Car 7211 at Clark and Irving Park in September 1957.
Charles L. Tauscher Photo/Wien-Criss Archive

Car 7189 on Clark just south of Irving Park by the Wunders Cemetery (on the right) in July 1957.
Charles L. Tauscher Photo/Wien-Criss Archive

Car 4109 on Clark at Seminary crossing the Milwaukee Road tracks in April 1954.
Bernard A. Rossbach Photo

Car 7164 on Clark at Seminary crossing the Milwaukee Road track in July 1957 with Wrigley Field at the left.
Charles L. Tauscher Photo/Wien-Criss Archive

Car 7178 on Clark at Seminary crossing the Milwaukee Road tracks in September 1957, just before streetcar service was cut back to Kinzie. The transportation scene may have been changing on the North Side, but not the Cubs, who finished tied for last place.
Charles L. Tauscher Photo/Wien-Criss Archive

Car 7190 side view at Clark and Seminary with Wrigley Field in the background in July 1957.
Charles L. Tauscher Photo/Wien-Criss Archive

Car 7222 at Clark and Seminary at the Milwaukee Road crossing with Wrigley Field in the background in July 1957. Back then a visit from the New York team meant the Giants, not the Mets.
Charles L. Tauscher Photo/Wien-Criss Archive

Car 7265 at Clark and Seminary at the Milwaukee Road crossing in April 1954.
Bernard A. Rossbach Photo

Car 4407 crossing the Milwaukee Road at Clark and Seminary in August 1957.
Thomas H. Desnoyers Photo/Krambles-Peterson Archive

Car 7178 at Clark and Roscoe in August 1957 with converted 6000 series Rapid Transit cars above.
Thomas H. Desnoyers Photo/Krambles-Peterson Archive

Car 7143 at Clark and Roscoe in August 1957.
Thomas H. Desnoyers Photo/Krambles-Peterson Archive

Car 7180 at Clark and Belmont in September 1957.
Charles L. Tauscher Photo/Wien-Criss Archive

Car 7163 at Clark, Halsted and Barry in July 1957.
Charles L. Tauscher Photo/Wien-Criss Archive

Car 7170 at Clark and Diversey in September 1957.
Charles L. Tauscher Photo/Wien-Criss Archive

Car 7143 inside Limits Station at Clark and Schubert in September 1957.
Kenneth J. Spengler Photo

Car 7151 coming out of the Limits Station at Clark and Schubert in September 1957.
Robert W. Gibson Photo/Electric Railway Historical Society Collection

Car 7211 at Clark and Schubert in September 1957.
Charles L. Tauscher Photo/Wien-Criss Archive

Car 7219 at Clark and Schubert in September 1957.
Robert W. Gibson Photo/Electric Railway Historical Society Collection

Car 4375 at Clark and Drummond in September 1957 with the Lakeview Post Office in background.
Charles L. Tauscher Photo/Wien-Criss Archive

173

Car 7211 at Clark and Drummond in September 1957 with Lakeview Post Office in background.
Charles L. Tauscher Photo/Wien-Criss Archive

Car 4373 at Clark and Belden in April 1955.
CERA Archives

Car 4166 at Clark and Lincoln Park West in November 1953.
Raymond DeGroote Photo

Car 4252 at Clark and Armitage in June 1948. Note the lack of a CTA logo.
George Krambles Photo/Krambles-Peterson Archive

Car 4384 at Clark and Armitage in September 1957.
Charles L. Tauscher Photo/Wien-Criss Archive

Car 4374 at Clark and Wells in September 1957.
Charles L. Tauscher Photo/Wien-Criss Archive

Car 7109 at Clark and Wells in November 1953.
Raymond DeGroote Photo

Car 7162 at Clark and LaSalle Drive in September 1957.
Charles L. Tauscher Photo/Wien-Criss Archive

Car 4401 on Clark north of North Avenue with the Plaza Hotel in the background in August 1957.
Robert W. Gibson Photo/Electric Railway Historical Society Collection

Car 4408 at Clark and North in April 1957 with the Chicago Historical Society (now Chicago History Museum) in the background.
Eugene Van Dusen Photo

Car 7201 at Clark and Germania Place in September 1957 with the Red Star Inn Restaurant on the left.
Robert W. Gibson Photo/Electric Railway Historical Society Collection

Car 7182 at Clark and Goethe in September 1957 prior to construction of Carl Sandburg Village.
Robert W. Gibson Photo/Electric Railway Historical Society Collection

The end of streetcar operation north of the loop was fast approaching as Car 7141 headed south at Clark and Schiller in September 1957.
Robert W. Gibson Photo/Electric Railway Historical Society Collection

Car 7148 at Clark and Division in September 1957.
Robert W. Gibson Photo/Electric Railway Historical Society Collection

Car 7216 at Clark and Delaware by Washington Square Park (aka Bughouse Square) in September 1957.
Robert W. Gibson Photo/Electric Railway Historical Society Collection

Car 7220 at Clark and Delaware by Washington Square Park (Bughouse Square) in September 1957.
Charles L. Tauscher Photo/Wien-Criss Archive

Car 7148 at Clark and Delaware in September 1957.
Robert W. Gibson Photo/Electric Railway Historical Society Collection

Car 4377 at Clark and Kinzie in September 1957.
Kenneth J. Spengler Photo

Car 7212 on Clark at the North Water Street bridge in June 1958.
Charles L. Tauscher Photo/Wien-Criss Archive

Car 4403 on Clark at the North Water Street "L" stub station in April 1958.
William C. Hoffman Photo/Wien-Criss Archive

Car 7213 on the Clark Street bridge over the Chicago River in May 1958.
Ronald J. Johnson Photo

Car 7139 at Clark and Wacker in April 1957.
William C. Janssen Photo/Krambles-Peterson Archive

Car 7205 at Clark and Lake as seen from the Clark & Lake "L" station in June 1958.
Charles L. Tauscher Photo/Wien-Criss Archive

Car 4408 at Clark and Lake in September 1957.
Robert W. Gibson Photo/Electric Railway Historical Society Collection

Car 4386 at Clark and Lake in June 1958. Note the Checker-built cabs operated by Yellow Cab Company.
Charles L. Tauscher Photo/Wien-Criss Archive

Car 7219 at Clark and Washington in front of the Cook County Building in June 1958.
Robert W. Gibson Photo/Electric Railway Historical Society Collection

Car 7072 at Madison and Dearborn due to a detour in November 1953.
Bernard A. Rossbach Photo

Car 7153 at Clark and Madison in June 1957.
Bernard L. Stone Photo/Krambles-Peterson Archive

Like the streetcars, local landmarks such as the Clark Theater and Wimpy ("The Glorified Hamburger") are just a memory. Here Car 7194 is passing Clark and Madison in August 1957.
William C. Hoffman Photo/Wien-Criss Archive

Car 7170 at Clark and Monroe in June 1957.
Bernard L. Stone Photo/Krambles-Peterson Archive

Car 4090 at Clark and Adams in May 1954 during rebuilding of Clark Street trackage.
Bernard A. Rossbach Photo

Car 7202 at Clark and Adams in May 1954 during rebuilding of Clark Street trackage to a southbound-only routing through the Loop.
Bernard A. Rossbach Photo

Car 7205 at Clark and Van Buren as seen from the LaSalle & Van Buren "L" station in June 1954 after Clark Street was made into a one-way street.
William C. Hoffman Photo/Wien-Criss Archive

Car 7264 at Clark and Van Buren with 4000 series "L" cars overhead in April 1956.
William C. Hoffman Photo/Wien-Criss Archive

Car 7210 at Clark and Van Buren in September 1957. The dome of the old Chicago Federal Building can be seen in the background.
Robert W. Gibson Photo/Electric Railway Historical Society Collection

Car 7219 at Clark and Congress in May 1958.
William C. Janssen Photo/Krambles-Peterson Archive

Car 7202 at Clark and Harrison in June 1958.
Charles L. Tauscher Photo/Wien-Criss Archive

Car 7207 at Clark and Harrison in June 1958.
Charles L. Tauscher Photo/Wien-Criss Archive

Car 4388 at Harrison and Dearborn in June 1958.
Charles L. Tauscher Photo/Wien-Criss Archive

Car 7209 at Harrison and Dearborn in June 1958.
William C. Janssen Photo/Krambles-Peterson Archive

Car 4363 at Dearborn and Harrison in March 1954.
Bernard A. Rossbach Photo

Car 7157 at Dearborn and Van Buren in June 1954 after Dearborn was made into a one-way street.
William C. Hoffman Photo/Wien-Criss Archive

Car 7192 at Dearborn and Monroe in October 1956.
William C. Janssen Photo/Krambles-Peterson Archive

Car 4384 at Dearborn and Lake with 6000 series "L" cars above in May 1958.
William C. Hoffman Photo/Wien-Criss Archive

Car 4157 at Dearborn and Lake during a parade reroute in November 1953.
Bernard A. Rossbach Photo

Car 4307 on the Dearborn Street bridge over the Chicago River in August 1953.
Bernard A. Rossbach Photo

Car 4377 at Dearborn and Kinzie in June 1958 with the future site of Harry Caray's restaurant in the background.
Kenneth J. Spengler Photo

Car 7208 turning off of Dearborn onto Kinzie in June 1958.
Charles L. Tauscher Photo/Wien-Criss Archive

Car 4390 at Kinzie and Clark with passengers boarding and alighting from car in June 1958.
CERA Archives

Car 7139 at Kinzie and Clark in November 1953 before the street was extensively repaved.
Bernard A. Rossbach Photo

Car 7200 at Kinzie and Clark in June 1958.
Charles L. Tauscher Photo/Wien-Criss Archive

Car 7121 at Clark and Taylor in July 1957, now the site of Dearborn Park.
William C. Hoffman Photo/Wien-Criss Archive

Clark and Taylor in April 1984 showing exposed streetcar rail during street construction.
Jeffrey L. Wien Photo/Wien-Criss Archive

Clark and Taylor in April 1984 showing exposed streetcar girder rail covered by several inches of asphalt.
Jeffrey L. Wien Photo/Wien-Criss Archive

Car 7224 and Car 7192 passing at Clark and Taylor in September 1957.
Robert W. Gibson Photo/Electric Railway Historical Society Collection

Car 4407 at Clark and Roosevelt in September 1957.
Robert W. Gibson Photo/Electric Railway Historical Society Collection

Car 7116 at the Museum Loop in April 1951 which was located at approximately Roosevelt Road and Lake Shore Drive. Short-turned Clark Street runs often used the Museum Loop until about 1952. The Museum Loop was located in what is now called the Museum Campus. Note Chicago Motor Coach buses in background.
Truman D. Heffner Photo/Krambles-Peterson Archive

Car 4408 at Clark and approximately 15th Street entering St. Charles Airline underpass in February 1958.
Charles L. Tauscher Photo/Wien-Criss Archive

Car 7077 at Clark near 15th Street going down the ramp of St. Charles Airline underpass in April 1954.
Bernard A. Rossbach Photo

Car 4380 at Clark and 16th passing under the St. Charles Airline overpass in June 1958.
Kenneth J. Spengler Photo

Car 4406 at Clark and 16th climbing up the ramp from St. Charles Airline overpass in October 1956.
William C. Hoffman Photo/Wien-Criss Archive

Car 7106 at Clark and 16th in August 1954.
William C. Hoffman Photo/Wien-Criss Archive

Car 4377 at Clark and 18th with St. John Church in the background in June 1957.
Robert W. Gibson Photo/Electric Railway Historical Society Collection

Car 4396 at Clark and Archer in June 1958.
Frank E. Butts Photo/Krambles-Peterson Archive

Car 7187 at Clark and Archer in May 1958.
Frank E. Butts Photo/Krambles-Peterson Archive

Car 7260 turning off of Clark onto Archer in April 1954.
Bernard A. Rossbach Photo

Car 7210 turning off of Clark onto Archer in October 1957 with New York Central "E" units in the background.
William C. Hoffman Photo/Wien-Criss Archive

Chicago Surface Lines supervisors' shanty at Clark and Archer in August 1957.
William C. Hoffman Photo/Wien-Criss Archive

Car 7204 on Archer turning onto Clark in August 1957 with New York Central "E" units overhead.
Charles L. Tauscher Photo/Wien-Criss Archive

Car 7223 at Archer and Wentworth in February 1958 with the last of the old style safety island light standards in view.
Charles L. Tauscher Photo/Wien-Criss Archive

Car 4341 at Wentworth and Cermak in November 1953.
Bernard A. Rossbach Photo

Car 4391 turning off of Cermak onto Clark in June 1958. Note "Museum" destination sign in error.
Frank E. Butts Photo/Krambles-Peterson Archive

Car 4399 turning off of Cermak onto Clark in October 1958.
William C. Hoffman Photo/Wien-Criss Archive

Car 4391 at Wentworth and 22nd Place in June 1958 with the famous Chinatown landmark Pui Tak Center Building to the left in the photo.
Charles L. Tauscher Photo/Wien-Criss Archive

Car 4376 at Wentworth near 35th in June 1958 with Comiskey Park off to the left.
Charles L. Tauscher Photo/Wien-Criss Archive

Car 4380 along South Wentworth Avenue in June 1958.
Charles L. Tauscher Photo/Wien-Criss Archive

Car 4397 at Wentworth and 40th in June 1957 with Stateway Gardens housing project in the background.
Robert W. Gibson Photo/Electric Railway Historical Society Collection

Flxible Twin Coach propane bus 5957 at Princeton and 47th in November 1959. This type of bus was used to replace many PCC operated car lines in the 1950s.
Charles L. Tauscher Photo/Wien-Criss Archive

Car 4404 at Wentworth and 51st in June 1958 with Rock Island Railroad buildings on the right side of the photo.
Robert W. Gibson Photo/Electric Railway Historical Society Collection

Car 7191 at Wentworth and 51st in June 1958.
Robert W. Gibson Photo/Electric Railway Historical Society Collection

Car 4396 at Wentworth and Garfield Blvd in June 1958.
Robert W. Gibson Photo/Electric Railway Historical Society Collection

Car 4393 at Wentworth near 59th Street in April 1958 approaching the Englewood "L" Wentworth Station from the south with converted 6000 series Rapid Transit cars above in the station.
William C. Hoffman Photo/Wien-Criss Archive

Car 4376 at Wentworth and 59th as seen from the Wentworth Station of the Englewood "L" in June 1958. In the early 1960s the area was demolished to make room for the Dan Ryan Expressway and would be unrecognizable today.
Thomas H. Desnoyers Photo/Krambles-Peterson Archive

Car 4372 at Wentworth and 59th as seen from the Wentworth Station of the Englewood "L" in June 1957.
Robert W. Gibson Photo/Electric Railway Historical Society Collection

Car 4353 at Wentworth and 60th during track repairs in October 1954 looking south from the Wentworth Englewood 'L Station.
William C. Hoffman Photo/Wien-Criss Archive

Car 7192 at Wentworth and 62nd in June 1958.
Charles L. Tauscher Photo/Wien-Criss Archive

Car 7191 on Wentworth just north of 63rd Street passing underneath the Pennsylvania Railroad underpass with a PRR Trainmaster diesel above in June 1958.
Kenneth J. Spengler Photo

Car 7194 at Wentworth and 63rd in June 1958.
Charles L. Tauscher Photo/Wien-Criss Archive

Car 7216 at Wentworth and 63rd Place in June 1958.
Kenneth J. Spengler Photo

Car 7219 at Wentworth and 65th in June 1957.
Robert W. Gibson Photo/Electric Railway Historical Society Collection

Car 7192 on South Wentworth Avenue in June 1958.
Robert W. Gibson Photo/Electric Railway Historical Society Collection

Car 7195 on South Wentworth Avenue in June 1957.
Robert W. Gibson Photo/Electric Railway Historical Society Collection

Car 7183 at Wentworth and 65th in May 1958.
Charles L. Tauscher Photo/Wien-Criss Archive

221

Car 7182 at Wentworth and 69th in June 1958.
Charles L. Tauscher Photo/Wien-Criss Archive

Car 4407 at Wentworth, Vincennes and 73rd intersection in June 1958.
Kenneth J. Spengler Photo

Car 7182 at Wentworth, Vincennes and 73rd intersection in June 1958.
Robert W. Gibson Photo/Electric Railway Historical Society Collection

Car 7195 at Vincennes and 77th in April 1958.
Charles L. Tauscher Photo/Wien-Criss Archive

Lineup of cars at 77th Street Station (carbarn) in September 1953.
Bernard A. Rossbach Photo

77th Street Station (carbarn) alley in June 1955.
Bernard A. Rossbach Photo

Car 4372 at Vincennes and 78th in May 1958.
Charles L. Tauscher Photo/Wien-Criss Archive

Car 7224 at Vincennes and 78th in April 1958.
Charles L. Tauscher Photo/Wien-Criss Archive

225

"Streetcars Turning" sign at Vincennes and 79th in May 1956. Note the lineup of PCCs in the distant background.
William C. Hoffman Photo/Wien-Criss Archive

Car 4398 at Vincennes and 79th in June 1958. Note overhead wire still up on 79th Street crossing Vincennes. At one time CTA had planned to convert 79th Street into a trolley bus line but it never came to pass.
Robert W. Gibson Photo/Electric Railway Historical Society Collection

Car 7216 laying over in the Vincennes-80th Loop in June 1958.
Charles L. Tauscher Photo/Wien-Criss Archive

Car 4372 at Vincennes and 80th in June 1958.
Kenneth J. Spengler Photo

Car 4372 entering Vincennes-80th Loop in June 1958.
Charles L. Tauscher Photo/Wien-Criss Archive

Car 4060 laying over in the Vincennes-80th Loop in July 1954. Note the old Divco milk truck.
Kenneth J. Spengler Photo

Car 4082 turning off of 81st onto Vincennes in April 1954.
Bernard A. Rossbach Photo

Car 4384 on Vincennes near 81st in May 1958.
William C. Janssen Photo/Krambles-Peterson Archive

Car 4396 turning off of Vincennes onto 81st in June 1958.
Charles L. Tauscher Photo/Wien-Criss Archive

Car 4384 at 81st and Normal in May 1958.
William C. Janssen Photo/Krambles-Peterson Archive

Car 4392 at 81st and Normal in June 1958.
Charles L. Tauscher Photo/Wien-Criss Archive

Car 4337 at 81st and Wallace in December 1953.
Bernard A. Rossbach Photo

Car 4077 at 81st and Wallace in March 1954.
William C. Janssen Photo/Krambles-Peterson Archive

Car 4401 at 81st and Wallace in June 1958.
Charles L. Tauscher Photo/Wien-Criss Archive

Car 4397 at 81st and Wallace in June 1958.
Charles L. Tauscher Photo/Wien-Criss Archive

Car 4296 passing Car 4213 at 81st and Halsted in October 1952.
George Krambles Photo/Krambles-Peterson Archive

Car 7149 at 81st and Halsted in June 1957.
Charles L. Tauscher Photo/Wien-Criss Archive

Car 7191 at 81st and Halsted in June 1958.
Robert W. Gibson Photo/Electric Railway Historical Society Collection

Cars 4284 and 7091 at 81st and Halsted in March 1950.
Robert W. Gibson Photo/Electric Railway Historical Society Collection

Car 7210 on Halsted at 81st on the wye in June 1957.
Charles L. Tauscher Photo/Wien-Criss Archive

CLARK WENTWORTH
NOV 9
Broadway-State
STAMP HERE
SEE OTHER SIDE
321883
TRANSFER NOT GOOD ON SURFACE DIVISION AFTER USING RAPID TRANSIT DIVISION UNLESS THE TIME IS STAMPED ON TRANSFER

36 119-MORGAN
4361
194

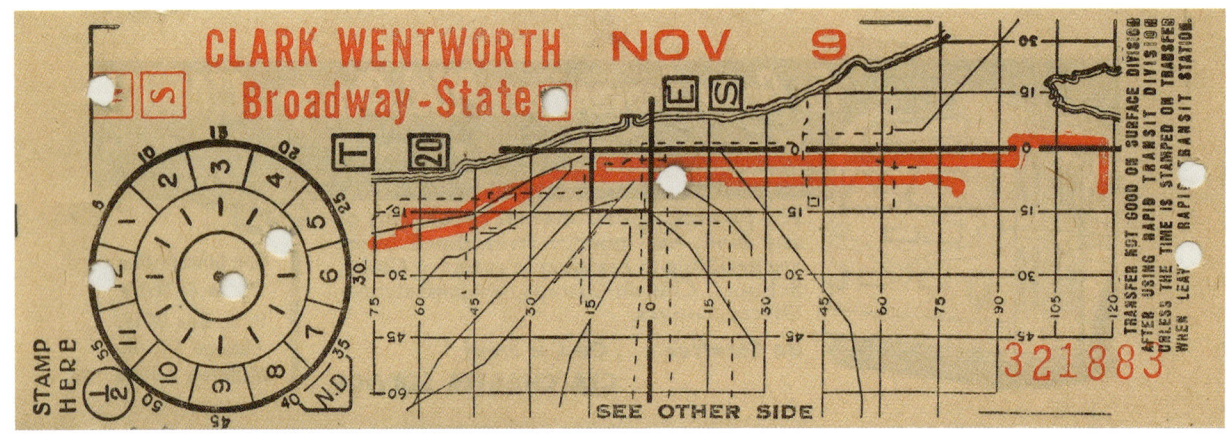

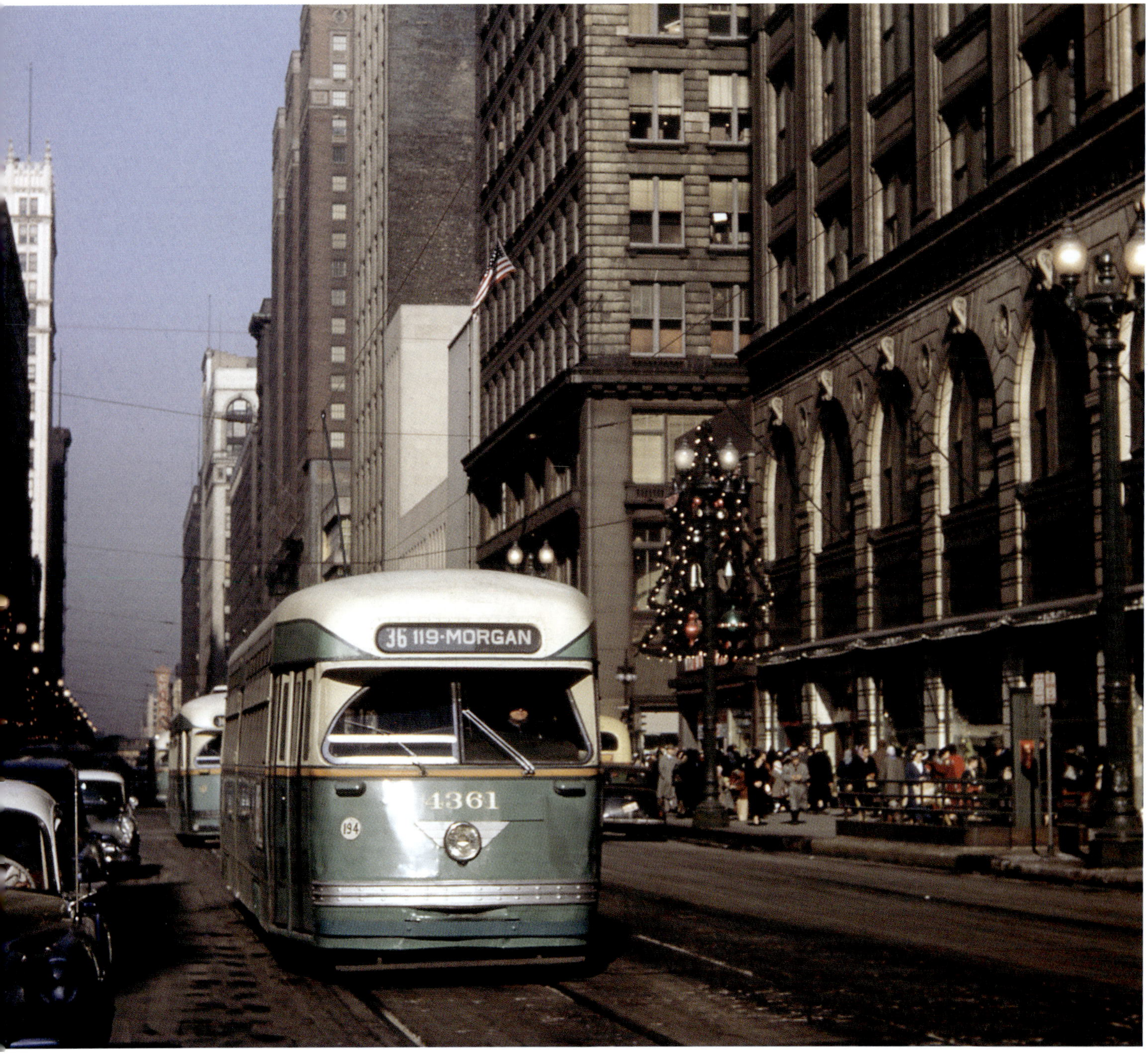

Route 36: Broadway/State

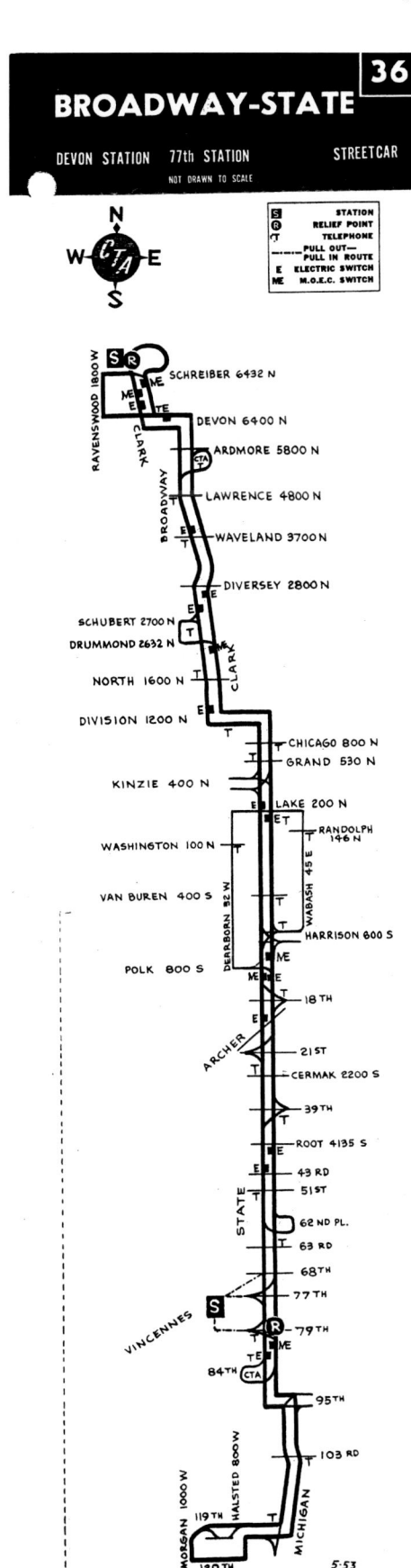

PCC Operations History

December 12, 1947
PCCs gradually placed in service; route becomes all-PCC in 1948.

December 15, 1947
Route cut back via Devon to Clark-Schreiber loop.

May 28, 1949
PCCs rerouted over new State Street Bridge.

September 5, 1954
Buses substituted for streetcars on weekends.

December 3, 1955
Through service discontinued. Streetcars replaced by buses on State Street section; other section becomes Route 36 Broadway operated by PCCs.

February 16, 1957
PCC cars replaced by buses.

Car 7113 at Devon and Ravenswood in April 1954.
Raymond DeGroote Photo

Car 7254 at Schreiber and Ravenswood in June 1954. The adjacent Chicago & North Western Railway embankment afforded the photographer an excellent view of trackage by the Devon Station (carbarn).
Robert W. Gibson Photo/Electric Railway Historical Society Collection

Car 7270 laying over at the Clark-Arthur Loop in April 1954. The Clark-Arthur Loop was used both by Clark-Wentworth and Broadway-State cars.
Bernard A. Rossbach Photo

Car 7205 on Clark just south of Schreiber in July 1951. The car was painted in the new CTA livery of Everglade Green and Cream.
William C. Hoffman Photo/Wien-Criss Archive

Car 4159 at Clark and Devon in May 1951.
Raymond DeGroote Photo

Car 7052 turning off of Clark onto Devon in April 1954.
Bernard A. Rossbach Photo

Car 7177 turning off of Clark onto Devon in July 1956. Chicagoans still had a large selection of local brews to choose from, including "Cheery Beery Edelweiss," as shown on the billboard in the background.
James J. Buckley Photo/CERA Archives

Car 7166 turning off of Clark onto Devon in February 1957, in the last days of the Broadway car line.
Charles L. Tauscher Photo/Wien-Criss Archive

Car 7069 at Devon and Clark in 1954, posing alongside a Fageol Twin Coach propane bus. While the Ridge Theater is long gone, a hardware store occupies the building today.
Bernard A. Rossbach Photo

PCC 7148 at Broadway and Devon in August 1956. The Howard "L" is visible in the background.
William C. Hoffman Photo/Wien-Criss Archive

Car 7170 and 7165 pass each other on Broadway south of Granville in 1956.
CERA Archives

Car 7260 on Broadway at Ardmore in April 1954. A short-turn loop was located to the right. What appears to be a car barn in the background actually was. It was built in 1893, but was out of use by 1914.
Raymond DeGroote Photo

Car 7156 at Broadway and Lawrence on February 15, 1957, the last full day of streetcar service on Broadway. *Giant* was playing at the Uptown Theater.
Charles L. Tauscher Photo/Wien-Criss Archive

Car 7193 at Broadway and Leland in August 1956, passing under the Howard "L".
William C. Hoffman Photo/Wien-Criss Archive

Car 7157 at Broadway and Wilson in July 1956.
Charles L. Tauscher Photo/CERA Archives

Car 7138 at Wilson and Broadway in October 1956. Even by 1956, Arthur U. Gerber's Beaux Arts "L" station at Wilson and Broadway still looked very close to the way it appeared when it opened in 1923. The wooden "L" cars seen in the photo were retired in late 1957.
Robert W. Gibson Photo/Electric Railway Historical Society Collection

Car 7077 at Broadway and Irving Park in June 1954.
Bernard A. Rossbach Photo

Car 7136 at Broadway where it intersects Halsted and Grace in the Fall of 1956. The Vogue Theater (opened as the Chateau Theater) closed two years later, and the site was later occupied by a tall, subsidized housing structure.
Robert W. Gibson Photo/Electric Railway Historical Society Collection

Car 4304 at Broadway, Halsted and Grace in June 1952. The rail and wire connections to Halsted street were still in place at the time this photo was taken.
Robert W. Gibson Photo/Electric Railway Historical Society Collection

Car 7148 at Broadway and Clarendon in the fall of 1956.
Robert W. Gibson Photo/Electric Railway Historical Society Collection

Car 7175 at Broadway and Cornelia in the fall of 1956. The tall spire in the background is part of the Lakeview Presbyterian Church at Addison.
Robert W. Gibson Photo/Electric Railway Historical Society Collection

Car 7219 at Broadway and Wellington in October 1956. The Barry-Regent Cleaners were already in operation at the time the photo was taken.
Jeffrey L. Wien Photo/Wien-Criss Archive

Car 7167 at Broadway and Wellington in October 1956, looking south.
Jeffrey L. Wien Photo/Wien-Criss Archive

Car 7250 at Broadway and Surf in June 1953. Located just a few doors east on Surf were the Britton I. Budd apartments, a desirable address for any Chicago traction enthusiast.
Robert W. Gibson Photo/Electric Railway Historical Society Collection

Car 7145 at the intersection of Clark, Broadway, and Diversey, in June 1954.
Robert W. Gibson Photo/Electric Railway Historical Society Collection

Car 4340 at Clark and Lincoln Park West in November 1953.
Raymond DeGroote Photo

Car 4267 at Clark and North in July 1950. The Chicago Historical Society building (now the Chicago History Museum) is seen in the background.
John Bromley Collection

Car 7205 at Division and Clark in August 1956.
William C. Hoffman Photo/Wien-Criss Archive

Car 7153 at State and Oak in September 1954. A route 70 Division Fageol Twin Coach bus is following behind.
William C. Janssen Photo/Krambles-Peterson Archive

Car 7188 at State and Walton in January 1957. Holy Name Cathedral can be seen to the south.
Robert W. Gibson Photo/Electric Railway Historical Society Collection

Car 7217 at State and Chicago in the fall of 1956.
Robert W. Gibson Photo/Electric Railway Historical Society Collection

Car 7126 at State and Chicago in May 1952.
Krambles-Peterson Archive

Car 7202 at State and Grand in the fall of 1956. To the right of the PCC is a Flxible Twin Coach propane bus running on route 36A State Street.
Robert W. Gibson Photo/Electric Railway Historical Society Collection

Car 7154 at State and Grand in March 1956. In the background, one sees an ACF-Brill trolley bus from Route 65 Grand Avenue, making a short-turn onto State Street.
Robert W. Gibson Photo/Electric Railway Historical Society Collection

Car 7223 at Wabash and Kinzie in May 1954, running on a diversion.
Bernard A. Rossbach Photo

Car 7125 at State and Kinzie in January 1954. Note new streetcar track construction in foreground.
William C. Janssen Photo/Krambles-Peterson Archive

Car 4348 on the State Street bridge in August 1953.
William C. Hoffman Photo/Wien-Criss Archive

Car 4152 on the State Street bridge in 1954, on its way to 119th and Morgan.
William C. Janssen Photo/Krambles-Peterson Archive

The full length of the State Street bridge is revealed in this August 1953 photo by Bill Hoffman. This deck truss bascule bridge was dedicated in 1949 and known officially as the Bataan-Corregidor Memorial Bridge.
William C. Hoffman Photo/Wien-Criss Archive

Car 7193 crossing Wacker Drive after leaving the State Street bridge in March 1956. To the right, the then-new Chicago Sun-Times Building was under construction. The site is now occupied by the Trump International Hotel and Tower.
Krambles-Peterson Archive

Car 7065 leaving the State Street bridge at Wacker Drive in March 1951.
Eugene Van Dusen Photo/Strahorn Library, Illinois Railway Museum

Car 7039 at State Street and Wacker Drive in August 1953.
William C. Hoffman Photo/Wien-Criss Archive

Car 7202 at State and Wacker in December 1956. Just ahead is Fritzel's, a restaurant where notables from politics, entertainment, and sports were known to congregate.
Robert W. Gibson Photo/Electric Railway Historical Society Collection

When this photo was taken in March 1954 of Car 7257 on State at Lake, the Loop was still a premier locale for evening dining and entertainment. Perhaps the two ladies in front of the car have just alighted and will cross the street to see *It Should Happen to You* with Judy Holliday and Peter Lawford at the State-Lake Theater.
William C. Hoffman Photo/Wien-Criss Archive

Car 7136 pauses in front of the Chicago Theater in June 1954. The entertainment billed on the marquee recalls a time when one could view a first-run feature film plus a live stage show, all for the price of a single movie ticket.
Larry Kostka Photo/CERA Archives

Car 4174 near State and Lake in June 1954.
Bernard L. Stone Photo/Krambles-Peterson Archive

Car 7227 at State and Lake in February 1957, with the Chicago Theater on the right, and the State-Lake Theater on the left, and the State-Lake "L" station in the background.
Raymond DeGroote Photo

Car 4371 at State and Randolph in July 1952. Two Greyhound "Silversides" buses linger in front of the State-Lake Theater in the background.
Henry Stange Jr. Photo/Krambles-Peterson Archive

Car 7047 at State and Randolph in June 1954, passing the Marshall Field & Co. flagship store, on its way to 119th and Morgan.
William C. Hoffman Photo/Wien-Criss Archive

Car 7189 at State and Madison, in August 1956. Chicago, a city of superlatives, boasted not only the world's largest streetcar system, but claimed that the "world's busiest corner" was at State and Madison. Chicago based its street numbering system from this intersection. It's not quite that busy as car 7178 approaches southbound on State.
William C. Hoffman Photo/Wien-Criss Archive

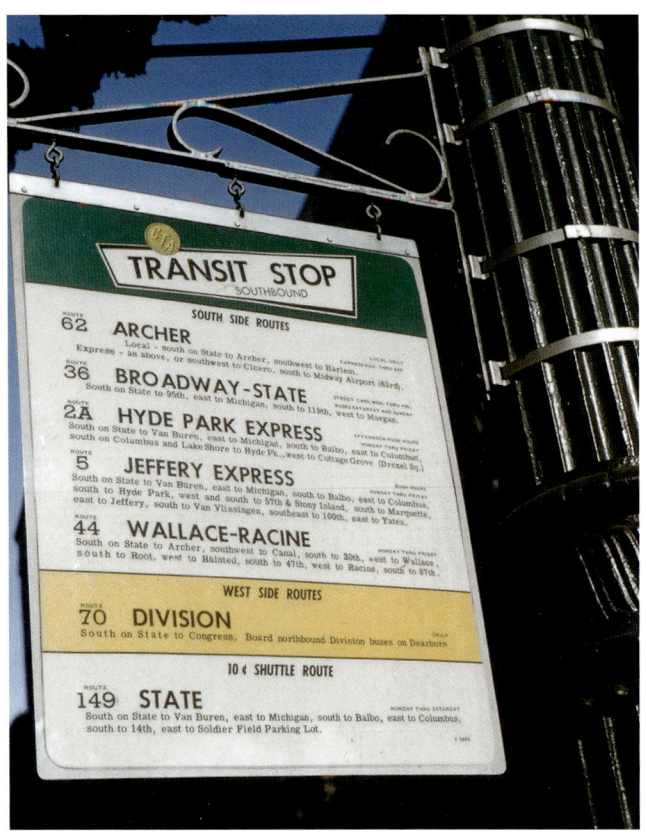

A view of the transit stop sign at State and Monroe from December 1954 shows one could still ride the entire length of Route 36 from Clark and Devon to 119th and Morgan, a distance of 25.6 miles one-way. *William C. Hoffman Photo/Wien-Criss Archive*

Car 7157 at State and Monroe in December 1956.
Robert W. Gibson Photo/Electric Railway Historical Society Collection

Car 4383 at State and Jackson in December 1954.
Raymond DeGroote Photo

Car 7213 at State and Jackson in December 1956. Streetcars ran past holiday decorations for one last season on State (at Jackson) in December 1956. For those who found the prices at Field's and Carson's too rich for their budgets, Goldblatt Brothers (right) offered a cheaper alternative.
Robert W. Gibson Photo/Electric Railway Historical Society Collection

Car 4361 at State and Jackson in December 1953.
James J. Buckley Photo/CERA Archives

Car 7240 at State and Van Buren in June 1954. Note the route 62 Archer Avenue White bus in the background, in the Mercury Green color scheme. This photo was taken from the State and Van Buren "L" station.
William C. Hoffman Photo/Wien-Criss Archive

Car 7200 at State and Van Buren in February 1957, taken from the State and Van Buren "L" station.
Raymond DeGroote Photo

Cars 7062 and 4091 at State and Van Buren in November 1954.
William C. Hoffman Photo/Wien-Criss Archive

Car 7142 at State and Van Buren in April 1955. State Street was a thriving commercial area and traffic could be very congested. This scene shows both prewar and postwar PCCs running amidst CTA buses (one still in Chicago Motor Coach colors).
William C. Janssen Photo/Krambles-Peterson Archive

Car 7242 at State and Van Buren in April 1955. This photo clearly demonstrates the PCCs ability to swallow large crowds.
William C. Janssen Photo/Krambles-Peterson Archive

Car 4263 at State and Van Buren in August 1953. A sales event titled "College Days" was under way on State Street.
William C. Hoffman Photo/Wien-Criss Archive

Car 7192 at State and Van Buren, passing underneath the "L" station in August 1956.
William C. Hoffman Photo/Wien-Criss Archive

Same location looking north as car 7271 runs south in August 1954.
William C. Hoffman Photo/Wien-Criss Archive

Car 7150 on State turning west on Polk in April 1956. The southern end of Route 36 was converted to motor bus in December 1955.
William C. Hoffman Photo/Wien-Criss Archive

Car 7162 at State and Polk in April 1956. Note the Flxible Twin Coach propane bus No. 5769 on Route 36A, with the destination sign 119th-Morgan, the former southern terminal of the Broadway-State car line.
William C. Hoffman Photo/Wien-Criss Archive

Car 7167 at State and Polk in November 1956.
Robert W. Gibson Photo/Electric Railway Historical Society Collection

Car 4406 on Polk near State in April 1956. The former Dearborn Street Station is in the background. Closed in 1971, the headhouse has been converted to offices and retail.
Krambles-Peterson Archive

Car 7193 at Polk and Dearborn in April 1956.
William C. Hoffman Photo/Wien-Criss Archive

Car 7139 at Dearborn just north of Lake Street in the spring of 1956.
Robert W. Gibson Photo/Electric Railway Historical Society Collection

273

Car 7105 at Dearborn and Wacker in May 1954. The freshly painted 7105, in Everglade Green and Cream, had been rerouted onto Dearborn, as State Street was being used for a parade that day.
Bernard A. Rossbach Photo

Car 7144 on the Dearborn Street bridge over the Chicago River, in August 1956.
William C. Hoffman Photo/Wien-Criss Archive

Car 7213 at Kinzie and Dearborn in May 1956. Just over two years later, the 7213 would make the last run ever by a Chicago streetcar.
Bernard L. Stone Photo/John Bromley Collection

Car 7177 at Kinzie and State in May 1956.
Robert W. Gibson Photo/Electric Railway Historical Society Collection

Car 7109 at State and 11th in June 1953, as seen from a window in the YMCA Hotel. View looking southwest.
CERA Archives

Car 4220 at State and Roosevelt in June 1951. One had the opportunity to view red streetcars and Green Hornets at the same time where State crossed under Roosevelt Road. The Roosevelt Road cars still ran west of Wabash.
Truman D. Hefner Photo/Krambles-Peterson Archive

Car 7214 at State and Roosevelt, as seen from the Roosevelt Road overpass.
Bernard A. Rossbach Photo

Car 7076 at State and Roosevelt in June 1953. Note the array of billboards in the background.
CERA Archives

Car 4323 at State and Roosevelt in October 1950, as seen from the Roosevelt road overpass. Note the street signs were still yellow.
William C. Hoffman Photo/Wien-Criss Archive

Car 4095 at State and 15th, in March 1954, as it passes a lineup of North Shore Line equipment stored on the "L" tracks south of Roosevelt Road.
Eugene Van Dusen Photo/Strahorn Library, Illinois Railway Museum

St. Louis-built car 7225 heads south at State and 15th in March 1954.
Bernard A. Rossbach Photo

Car 7144 at State and Cermak, in June 1953, taken from the Jackson Park-Englewood "L" Cermak Road station.
CERA Archives

Car 7267 at State and 33rd in January 1954. The Illinois Institute of Technology campus is in the background. Renowned architect Ludwig Mies van der Rohe began designing buildings for IIT in the 1940s in what became known as the "Mies Campus."
William C. Janssen Photo/Krambles-Peterson Archive

Car 4406 at State and 34th in October 1955.
William C. Hoffman Photo/Wien-Criss Archive

Car 7112 at State and 34th in January 1954. Note Comiskey Park in background, before the days of the Dan Ryan expressway and five years before then-owner Bill Veeck completely repainted the exterior brickwork white before the start of the 1960 season.
William C. Janssen Photo/Krambles-Peterson Archive

Car 7205 at State and 51st in December 1954. Note the trolley bus overhead crossing for the 51st-55th Street trolley bus line.
Michael Raia Collection

Andre Kristopans' Story

The whole incident was a series of unfortunate misunderstandings. The detour had been: south on State--reverse direction through the 62nd St. short-turn loop—north on State—west on 59th—south on Wentworth—east on 69th—south on State over regular route. As a result, the lever switch leading into the loop which normally would have to be opened by the conductor had been "plugged" into its reverse position. As the water had gone down in the underpass in question, the supervisor on scene had decided to end the reroute and allow cars to continue on the through routing. He apparently told the motorman of the last previous southbound car to tell this to the supervisor at 59th St to tell the next southbound he would be going straight. This the 59th supervisor did to the ill-fated car.

However, somebody forgot to return the 62nd St. Loop switch to normal, so it was still set for the curve into the Loop. The motorman on 7078 was told he was going straight, so he accelerated away from the stop at 61st (where a friend of mine got off!) and did not see the reversed switch until he was almost on top of it. The car swung left at a relatively high rate of speed (probably about 20-25 mph) and hit a northbound oil truck that just happened to be starting across the track. This was a straight truck hauling a two-axle full trailer. The PCC hit the truck just behind the cab, and punctured its fuel tank. This caused a plume of gasoline to come in thru the car's shattered windshield, which is what caused the fire on the car. The car derailed on impact and swung completely around until it was facing north and was east of the tracks. As I understand, the fuel truck was pretty much empty, but the fire from the fuel tank contents did cause the gasoline in the cargo tanks to blow up, which eventually burned down much of the block.

The charred shell of PCC 7078 at State and 62nd Place on May 25, 1950, after colliding with a gasoline truck.

Where the real problem came in was that at the time there were no emergency door releases, and when the car derailed and the pole came off the wire, the conductor's door controls went dead, so the doors were basically locked closed. Inward or outward opening doors would have made no difference. The big change was that afterwards, and to this day, every CTA vehicle has a VERY obvious door release, which on air-operated doors takes the air off the closing cylinder, and on electrically-operated doors pulls a pin that disengages the door from the closing mechanism. In other systems, you frequently have a cover of some sort that you need to break to operate an emergency release, but in Chicago they have always been fully exposed and very obvious, a red ball (or cherry as we call them).

Other PCC vs. Fuel Truck Accidents

In 1948, there were four incidents between Green Hornets and fuel trucks without any fatalities. A fuel truck carrying oil struck a streetcar on February 5th at 59th Street and Damen. Although the tanks were breached, the oil did not ignite. Five days later, another collision at 79th Street and Ashland resulted in four people being injured. Once again, the truck was carrying oil, and there was no fire.

On March 1st, a Green Hornet collided with a truck hauling gas on Western Avenue. This time, the fuel did ignite, but the car was almost empty and the nine people aboard exited safely through the rear doors. Then on October 26th, a Green Hornet rear-ended a gas truck at 63rd and State. The gasoline emptied into the sewers and, moments later, ignited. Only a pedestrian was injured.

Car 7144 at State and 62nd Place in November 1955, at the site of the infamous accident five years earlier.
William C. Hoffman Photo/Wien-Criss Archive

Car 7113 at State and 62nd Place in November 1955, affording a broader view of the site of the 1950 accident.
William C. Hoffman Photo/Wien-Criss Archive

Car 7105 lays over at the State-62nd Place Loop in 1954.
Bernard A. Rossbach Photo

Car 7154 at State and 63rd in November 1955. A view of the infamous viaduct whose flooding in May 1950 necessitated the southbound cars being cut back to the Loop at State and 62nd Place.
William C. Hoffman Photo/Wien-Criss Archive

Car 4228 at State and 64th in March 1948. In this photo brand new Green Hornet 4228 approaches the viaduct on a southbound run. There is neither a CSL nor a CTA logo in place, but CTA did affix a sign in front proclaiming that number 4228 was "Another New CTA Streetcar."
Michael Raia Collection

Car 7039 at State and 64th in March 1948, approaching the infamous viaduct. Note the CSL logo.
Michael Raia Collection

Car 7174 at State and 73rd in the fall of 1955. Note the billboard in the background, touting Ford's 1956 line of trucks.
Robert V. Mehlenbeck Photo/Krambles-Peterson Archive

Car 7204 at the State-84th Street Loop in April 1954. Note the Marshall Field & Co. branch store in the background. This site is now occupied by the Dan Ryan Expressway.
Bernard A. Rossbach Photo

Car 4132 at the State-84th Street Loop in October 1953. It was newly repainted in Everglade Green. This roof treatment was not applied to any other cars.
Bernard A. Rossbach Photo

Car 7138 at the State-84th Street Loop in February 1950.
Eugene Van Dusen Photo/Strahorn Library, Illinois Railway Museum

Car 4180 at State and 86th Street in May 1952.
John D. Koschawanez Photo/John Bromley Collection

Car 7204 at 95th and Michigan in May 1951. The one-man red car is operating on the 93rd-95th Street line.
John D. Koschawanez Photo/John Bromley Collection

Car 4248 at 95th and Michigan in May 1951. Despite being repainted in the new Everglade Green color scheme, the car still sported the old 1948 orange CTA logo.
George Krambles Photo/Krambles-Peterson Archive

Cars 4348 and 7218 meet at Michigan and 112th in the fall of 1952. This view was taken from the rooftop of J. C. Penney in what was then a bustling retail neighborhood.
Robert V. Mehlenbeck Photo/Krambles-Peterson Archive

Car 7171 at Michigan and 112th in the fall of 1954, shown in the heart of the Roseland shopping district.
Bernard A. Rossbach Photo

Car 7077 at Michigan and 119th in October 1953.
Bernard A. Rossbach Photo

Car 4340 at 119th and Princeton in October 1953.
Bernard A. Rossbach Photo

Car 4392 at 119th and Normal in March 1954. Note Walt Disney's *Living Desert* playing at the art moderne Normal Theater, which opened in 1936.
George Krambles Photo/Krambles-Peterson Archive

Car 7212 at 119th and Halsted in April 1954. The conductor is out flagging the car as it crosses the Pennsylvania Railroad's "Panhandle line."
William C. Hoffman Photo/Wien-Criss Archive

Car 7229 at 119th and Halsted crossing the PRR tracks in April 1954. Note gateman's tower.
William C. Hoffman Photo/Wien-Criss Archive

Car 7225 laying over at 119th and Morgan in August 1954.
William C. Hoffman Photo/Wien-Criss Archive

Car 4212 at 119th and Morgan in May 1948. So new, a CTA logo has yet to be applied.
Robert V. Mehlenbeck Photo/Krambles-Peterson Archive

Car 7271 at 119th and Morgan in March 1954. Cars are waiting for the northbound run to Clark and Devon.
Robert V. Mehlenbeck Photo/Krambles-Peterson Archive

Cars 7074 and 7229 at 119th and Morgan in October 1953.
Bernard A. Rossbach Photo

Car 7260 at 119th and Morgan in early morning of December 3, 1955, in the final hours of the Broadway-State car line.
William C. Janssen Photo/Krambles-Peterson Archive

Car 7107 at 119th and Morgan in June 1955 on a warm summer night.
CERA Archives

Car 4212 at Morgan and 119th in May 1948.
Robert V. Mehlenbeck Photo/Krambles-Peterson Archive

Car 4092 at Morgan and 119th in June 1952, as it began its 25.6 mile northbound journey to the Clark-Schreiber Loop.
Robert W. Gibson Photo/Electric Railway Historical Society Collection

Car 4392 at 120th and Morgan in March 1954, in the industrialized West Pullman neighborhood.
William C. Janssen Photo/Krambles-Peterson Archive

Car 4169 at Morgan and 119th in February 1952.
Eugene Van Dusen Photo/Strahorn Library, Illinois Railway Museum

Car 4068 at 120th and Halsted in March 1954. Note the "Hamm's- the Beer Refreshing" billboard in the background.
George Krambles Photo/Krambles-Peterson Archive

Car 4068 in March 1954, turning off of 120th into Halsted. Note the tracks in the foreground from the former Chicago & Interurban Traction Co.
William C. Janssen Photo/Krambles-Peterson Archive

Car 4068 at 120th and Halsted in March 1952, sporting the new CTA livery of Everglade Green and Cream.
Robert W. Gibson Photo/Electric Railway Historical Society Collection

Car 4132 on Halsted, approaching 119th in March 1954.
George Krambles Photo/Krambles-Peterson Archive

Car 4132 at Halsted and 119th in March 1954, with the conductor walking ahead to flag the streetcar over the PRR "Panhandle line."
William C. Janssen Photo/Krambles-Peterson Archive

Car 7238 on 119th and Halsted, crossing the PRR "Panhandle Line" in March 1952.
Robert W. Gibson Photo/Electric Railway Historical Society Collection

Car 7201 at Clark and Wells on February 16, 1957. This was the last car to operate on the Broadway car line and on State Street.
Charles H. Thorpe Photo/Wien-Criss Archive

HALSTED
DOWNTOWN
JUN 29
STAMP HERE
TRANSFER NOT GOOD ON SURFACE DIVISION AFTER USING RAPID TRANSIT DIVISION UNLESS THE TIME IS STAMPED ON TRANSFER WHEN LEAVING RAPID TRANSIT STATION.
698388

42 HALSTED-79
4280
7092

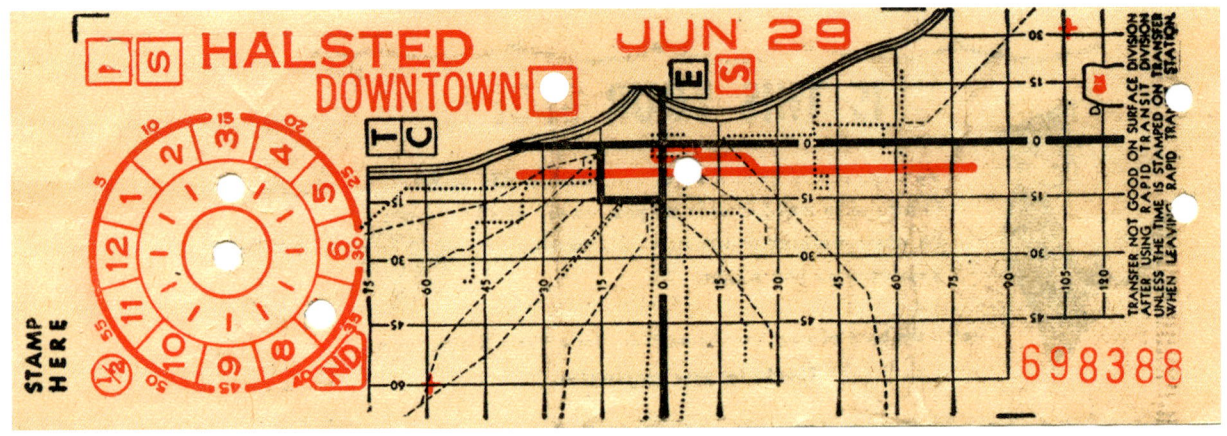

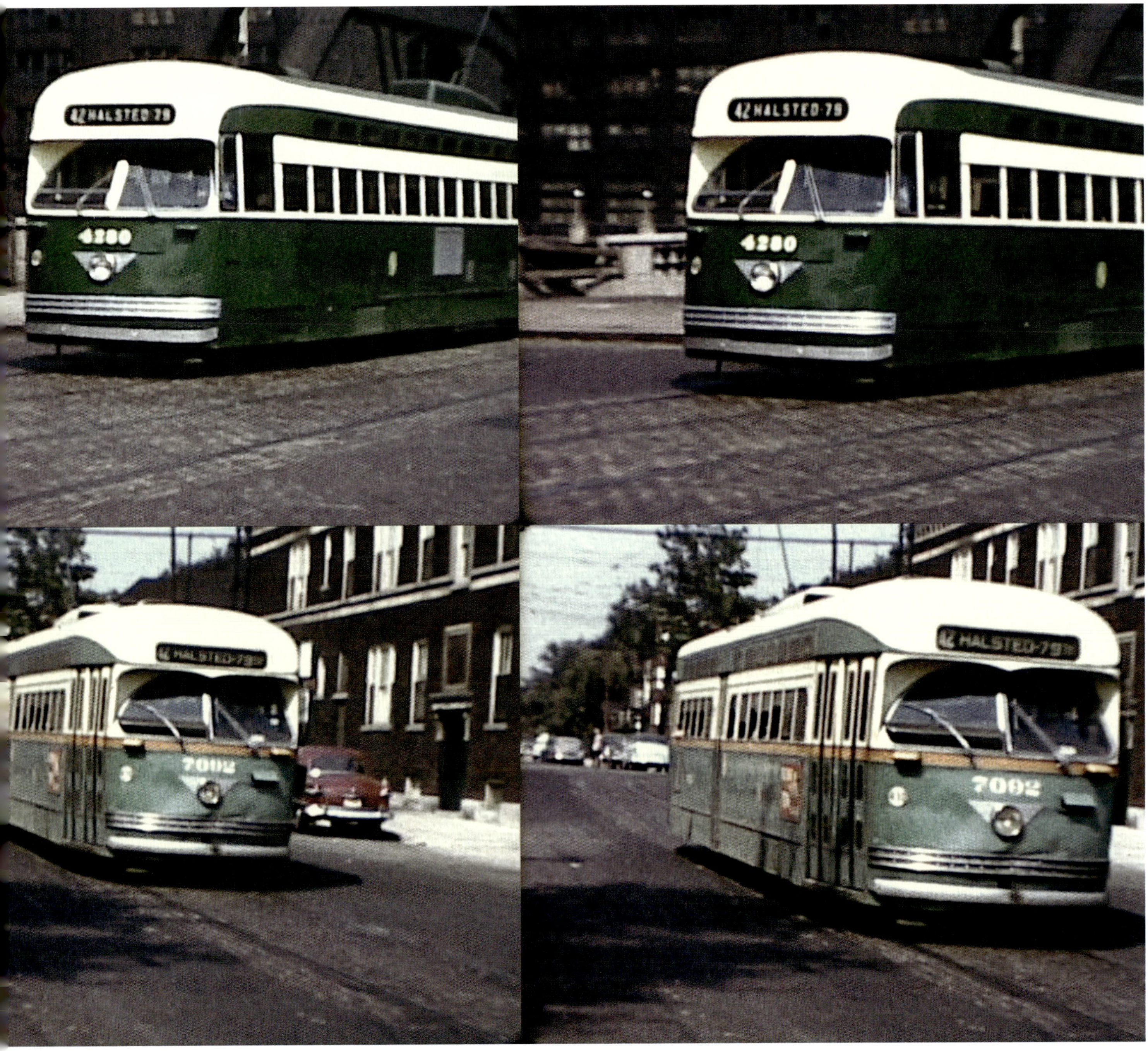

Route 42: Halsted/Downtown

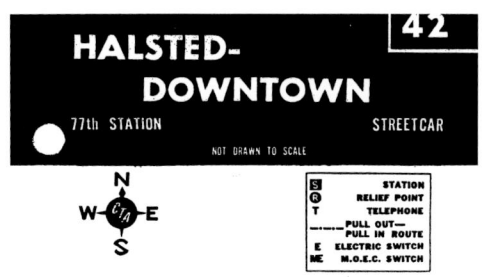

PCC Operations History

December 4, 1949
PCCs introduced to route; mixed operation with standard red cars. Service cut back to loop at 79th and Halsted.

July 1950
Some service operated by PCCs.

February 28, 1951
Northern terminal changed to Clark and Illinois from Clark and Chicago.

November 24, 1951
Bus operation on weekends replacing streetcars.

June 1953
Begin gradual replacement of PCC cars with standard red cars. Route operated exclusively by standard streetcars by end of 1953.

May 29, 1954
Streetcars replaced by buses on route.

Note: All photos in this section are frame captures from an 8 mm film.

Car 7092 running on Route 42 on Emerald south of 79th Street.

Car 4220 running on Route 42 Halsted-Downtown southbound on Clark Street at Wacker Drive after coming off of the Clark Street Bridge.

WESTERN
SEP 25
STAMP HERE
TRANSFER NOT GOOD ON SURFACE DIVISION AFTER USING RAPID TRANSIT DIVISION UNLESS THE TIME IS STAMPED ON TRANSFER WHEN LEAVING RAPID TRANSIT STATION
773523

RIVERVIEW
4060

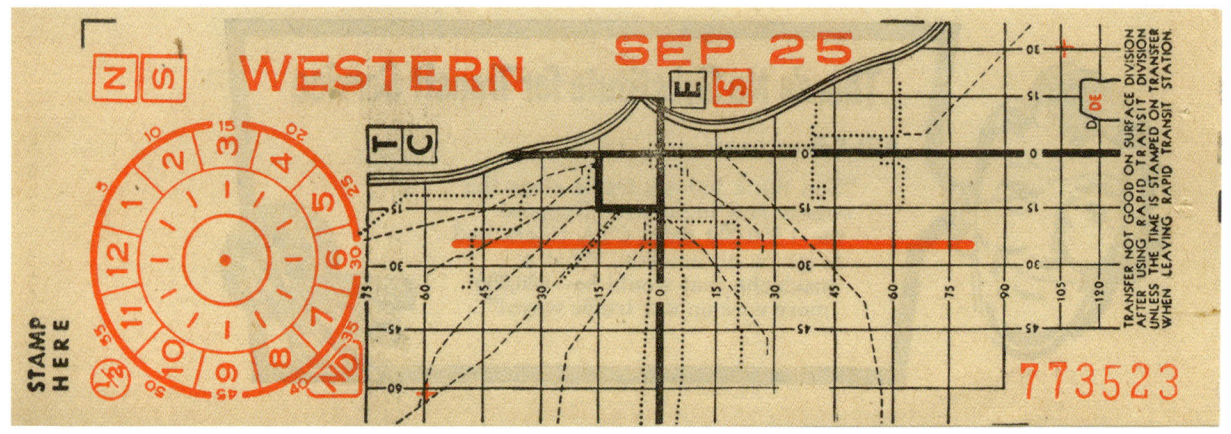

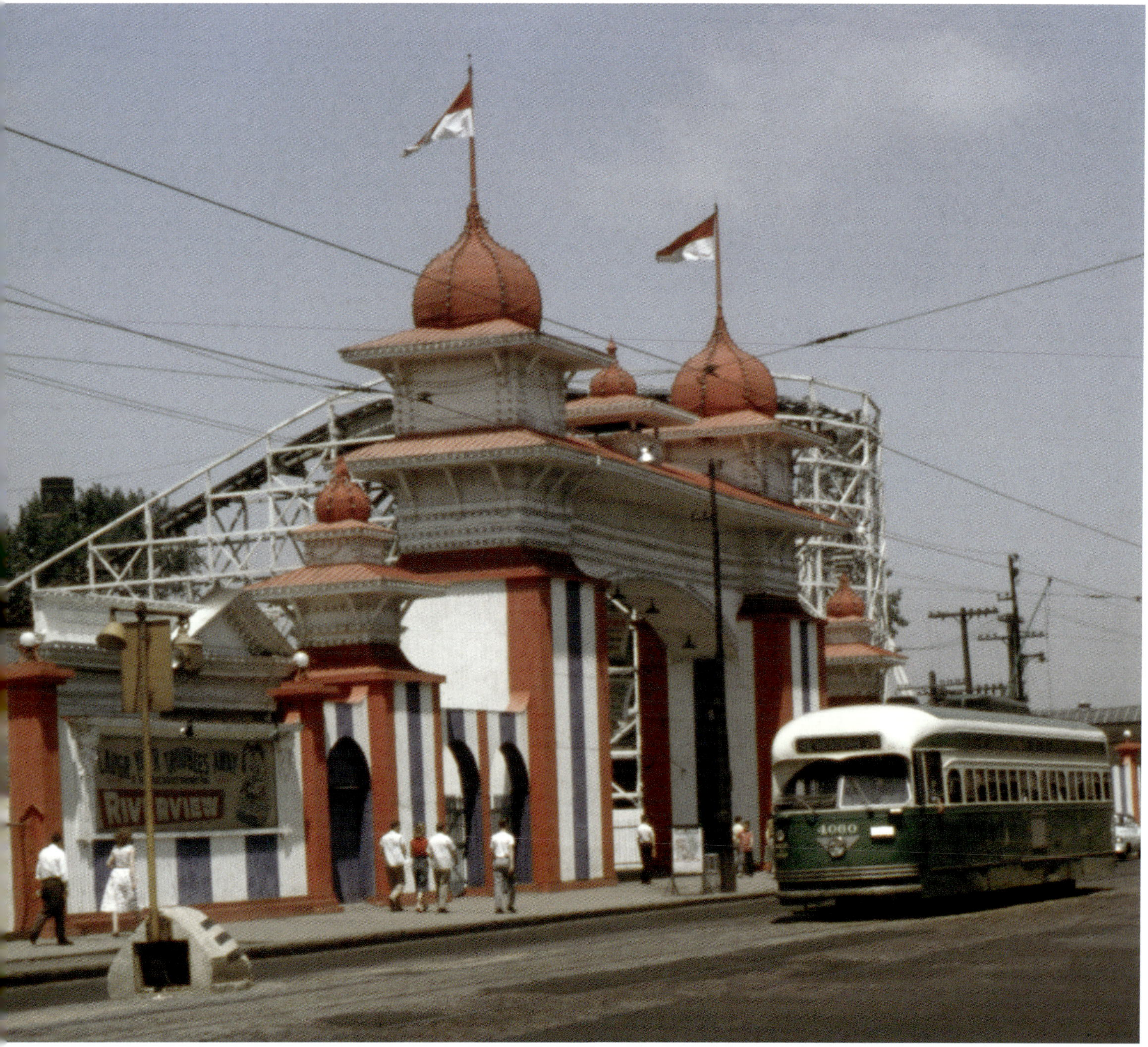

Route 49: Western

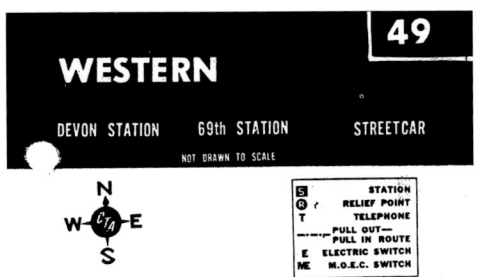

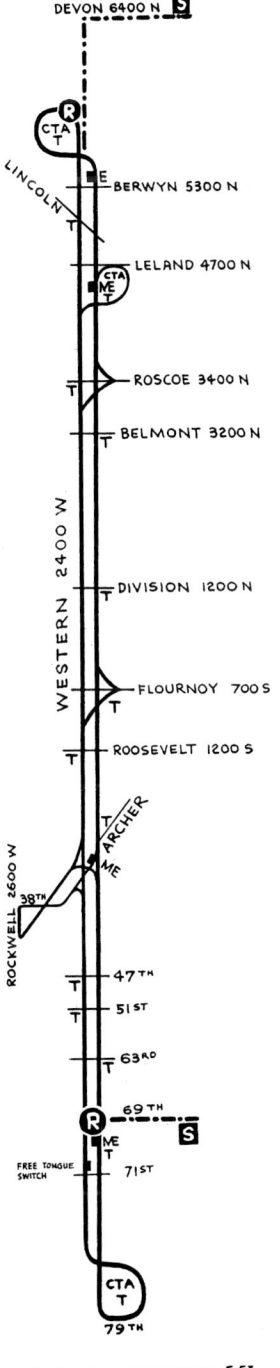

PCC Operations History

August 1, 1948
PCC service inaugurated with postwar cars. Service cut back from 111th and Western to 79th and Western. At this time the northern terminal was the loop at Clark and Schreiber.

December 12, 1948
Service in north cut back from Clark-Schreiber to Western-Berwyn.

December 7, 1952
Buses substituted for streetcars on weekends.

September 9, 1954
Transferred from 69th Street car barn to 77th Street station.

June 18, 1955
Weekend bus operation ends.

June 19, 1955
One-man operation begun with postwar PCCs and prewar PCCs brought up from Cottage Grove after that line was converted to buses. Streetcar operation reverted back to seven days a week.

June 17, 1956
Buses substituted for streetcars. Last day of operation of prewar PCCs.

Car 7115 at Devon and Ridge in May 1953, passing underneath the Chicago & North Western's Milwaukee Division. This car is a pull-out from the Devon Station.
Bernard L. Stone Photo/John Bromley Collection

Car 7117 at Devon and Claremont in April 1950. This car is a pull-out.
William C. Hoffman Photo/Wien-Criss Archive

Car 7005 at Devon and Claremont in June 15, 1956. The "not in service" sign on this prewar PCC indicated that this car was a pull-in to the Devon Station. No passengers were carried on northbound pull-ins. This photo was taken on the last full day of streetcar service on Western Avenue.
Raymond DeGroote Photo

Car 7258 at Western and Devon in June 1956. The "Enter at Front" sign indicated that this car was operating as a one-man PCC.
Raymond DeGroote Photo

Car 4383 at Western and Devon in August 1952.
George Krambles Photo/Krambles-Peterson Archive

Car 4039 at Western and Rosemont in June 1956. After the conversion of Cottage Grove to buses on June 18, 1955, the prewar cars were reassigned to Western Avenue where they operated for just under a year.
Raymond DeGroote Photo

Car 7036 at Western and Peterson in June 1956. This portion of Western was a virtual "automobile dealers row." The sign for longtime Chevy dealer "Z" Frank can be discerned in the background.
Raymond DeGroote Photo

Car 7259, three blocks north of the Western-Berwyn Loop at Bryn Mawr.
Raymond DeGroote Photo

Car 4374 at Western and Thorndale in August 1954. Rosehill Cemetery is immediately behind the car to the left.
Raymond DeGroote Photo

Car 7129 at Western and Thorndale in August 1954.
Raymond DeGroote Photo

Car 4054 approaching the Western-Berwyn Loop in March 1955, en route to 79th and Western.
Bernard A. Rossbach Photo

Car 7215 at the Western-Berwyn Loop in April 1952.
Krambles-Peterson Archive

Car 4376 at the Western-Berwyn Loop in September 1953, in the new CTA livery of Everglade Green and Cream.
Raymond DeGroote Photo

Car 7044 at Western and Berwyn in July 1955. Newly converted one-man, postwar car 7044 is about to turn into the Western-Berwyn Loop. Just a month earlier, the Western Avenue line had been converted to all one-man operation.
George Krambles Photo/Krambles-Peterson Archive

Car 7238 at Western and Farragut in June 1956.
Raymond DeGroote Photo

Car 7044 at Western and Foster in December 1955.
Raymond DeGroote Photo

315

Car 4405 at Western and Winnemac in June 1950.
Robert W. Gibson Photo/Electric Railway Historical Society Collection

Car 4397 at Western and Lincoln in June 1951. Note the Flxible Clipper bus operating on an American Coach Company route.
Robert W. Gibson Photo/Electric Railway Historical Society Collection

Car 4053 at Western and Leland in June 1956. Photo taken from the Western Avenue station of the Ravenswood "L" line (now the CTA Brown Line).
William C. Hoffman Photo/Wien-Criss Archive

Car 7003 at Western and Leland in June 1956. Two prewar PCCs are northbound, while an American Coach Co. suburban bus can be seen at left.
Raymond DeGroote Photo

Car 4045 at the Western-Leland Loop in June 1955. A Route 49B North Western Avenue Fageol Twin Coach propane bus is loading passengers in the loop.
Bernard A. Rossbach Photo

Car 7253 at Western and Leland in June 1956. The car has just passed under the Western Avenue station of the Ravenswood "L."
William C. Hoffman Photo/Wien-Criss Archive

Car 4006 at Western and Eastwood in June 1956.
Raymond DeGroote Photo

Car 4020 at Western and Montrose in November 1955. Welles Park is to the right.
Raymond DeGroote Photo

Car 4060 at Western and Roscoe in June 1956. Southbound PCC 4060 passes the entrance to Riverview Amusement Park at Roscoe in June 1956.
William C. Hoffman Photo/Wien-Criss Archive

Car 7245 at Western and Roscoe in July 1955. This car was passing the park's entrance on a northbound run. In the background is the famed Parachute Jump, a ride that provided a breathtaking—some would say terrifying-—view from its top.
Robert W. Gibson Photo/John Bromley Collection

Car 7255 crossing the Western Avenue bridge over the North Branch of the Chicago River in January 1956.
William C. Hoffman Photo/Wien-Criss Archive

Car 7037 emerges from the Western Avenue bridge over the North Branch of the Chicago River in June 1956.
William C. Hoffman Photo/Wien-Criss Archive

The trunnion-bascule bridge is archetypical of Chicago's moveable bridges. Here is how the bridge we have been viewing looks when it is raised. Photo from June 1956.
William C. Hoffman Photo/Wien-Criss Archive

Car 7259 at the intersection of Western and Milwaukee, with Armitage in the distance, in January 1956. This photo was taken from the Western Avenue station of the Logan Square "L" looking north. The Marmon trolley bus seen in the distance was operating on Route 73 Armitage.
William C. Hoffman Photo/Wien-Criss Archive

Car 4033 at Western and Milwaukee in June 1956. A southbound prewar PCC has just passed a northbound postwar "Green Hornet." In the foreground, we see a southbound Route 56 Milwaukee Avenue Fageol Twin Coach propane bus is heading south on Milwaukee Avenue.
William C. Hoffman Photo/Wien-Criss Archive

Car 4411 at Western at Milwaukee in early May 1952. Photo taken from the Western Avenue station of the Logan Square "L."
Bernard L. Stone Photo/Krambles-Peterson Archive

Car 7034 at Western and the Logan Square "L" in June 1956. A train of 4000-series "L" cars is stopped at the station.
William C. Hoffman Photo/Wien-Criss Archive

Car 4391 at Western and Winnebago in June 1952. The car is shown in the same colors it wears today at the Illinois Railway Museum in Union.
Bernard L. Stone Photo/Krambles-Peterson Archive

Car 4055 at Western and Winnebago in June 1956.
William C. Hoffman Photo/Wien-Criss Archive

Car 4373 at Western and Van Buren in June 1954. PCC streetcar 4373 waits for a two-car train of "flat door" 6000s to cross at the Garfield "L" tracks. The streetcar is operating on a shoo-fly while the new bridge over the Congress Street Expressway is being built.
William C. Hoffman Photo/Wien-Criss Archive

In October 1952, before Garfield "L" trains were relocated to ground level operation along Van Buren Street, northbound 7192 makes the stop at Western and Van Buren. This photo shows how the "Green Hornet" door arrangement enabled these cars to quickly load and unload passengers.
William C. Hoffman Photo/Wien-Criss Archive

Car 4378 at Western and Van Buren in October 1952. The Everglade Green paint scheme was being introduced at the time.
William C. Hoffman Photo/Wien-Criss Archive

At Western and Van Buren in 1953, Car 4385 waits for a two-car wooden Met "L" train to pass. "L" trains proceeded across grade crossings on authority of traffic signals only.
William C. Janssen Photo/Krambles-Peterson Archive

Car 7037 at Western and Van Buren on the new bridge over the Congress Street Expressway in September 1955.
Thomas H. Desnoyers Photo/Krambles-Peterson Archive

Car 7118 at Western and Van Buren in June 1956, approaching the bridge over the Congress Street Expressway.
Wien-Criss Archive

Car 7018 at Western and Van Buren in June 1956.
William C. Hoffman Photo/Wien-Criss Archive

Western and Congress in September 1955. A prewar PCC is shown on the new Western Avenue bridge over the Congress Street Expressway.
William C. Hoffman Photo/Wien-Criss Archive

Western and Congress in June 1956. By June 1956 portions of the expressway were open to traffic, and the laying of track for the new "L" line in the expressway median was evident.
William C. Hoffman Photo/Wien-Criss Archive

Car 7156 crosses the Van Buren surface trackage on a shoo-fly while the new expressway bridge was under construction. A Garfield Park "L" train waits for the PCC to pass and the traffic light to change.
William C. Hoffman Photo/Wien-Criss Archive

Car 4036 at Western and 21st in June 1956. This photo provides a good view of the typical safety island used by Chicago streetcars after World War II.
William C. Hoffman Photo/Wien-Criss Archive

Car 4044 at Western and 21st in June 1955.
William C. Hoffman Photo/Wien-Criss Archive

Car 7009 at Western and 21st in May 1956. The car has just passed underneath the Douglas Park "L."
Bernard A. Rossbach Photo

Car 7239 at Western and Cullerton in November 1955. This view from the "L" shows that when Western Avenue was widened in this area (circa 1927), the streetcar tracks remained offset, in their original location.
William C. Hoffman Photo/Wien-Criss Archive

Car 4393 at Western and 21st in July 1950. Note the Wrigley Company delivery truck.
William C. Hoffman Photo/Wien-Criss Archive

Car 4373 at Western and Cullerton in October 1953. Note two other southbound PCC cars following behind.
William C. Hoffman Photo/Wien-Criss Archive

Car 7213 at Western and Cullerton in July 1951. View taken from the Douglas Park "L."
William C. Hoffman Photo/Wien-Criss Archive

Car 4402 at Western and 21st in June 1954. The width of the postwar PCCs is aptly demonstrated by the narrow clearance between 4402 and another car.
William C. Hoffman Photo/Wien-Criss Archive

Car 4041 at Western and 24th in June 1956. This clearly demonstrates the offset nature of the streetcar tracks after Western Avenue was widened here in the 1920s.
William C. Hoffman Photo/Wien-Criss Archive

Car 7205 at Western and 26th in June 1956. The PCC seems lost amidst a sea of truck traffic as it picks its way south along Western.
William C. Hoffman Photo/Wien-Criss Archive

Car 4028 at Western and 27th in November 1955. This car has little traffic to impede its way at Western and 27th. The route in this area skirted the large McCormick Works of International Harvester that was once located at Western and Blue Island Avenue.
William C. Hoffman Photo/Wien-Criss Archive

Car 4059 at Western and 28th in November 1955.
William C. Hoffman Photo/Wien-Criss Archive

Car 4053 at Western and 31st in June 1956. The southbound streetcar has just crossed the imposing bridge at Western and 31st Street, which has since been replaced by a permanent span.
William C. Hoffman Photo/Wien-Criss Archive

At Western and 31st in August 1954. An overall view of the 31st Street vertical lift bridge over the Sanitary and Ship Canal with a PCC car crossing over it. Built with Public Works Administration funds, the structure was completed and dedicated in 1940.
William C. Hoffman Photo/Wien-Criss Archive

Car 7209 at Western and 31st leaving the bridge in February 1954.
Bernard A. Rossbach Photo

Car 4049 at Western and 33rd in May 1956. Car 4049 is about to cross the bridge over the Sanitary and Ship Canal.
William C. Janssen Photo/Krambles-Peterson Archive

Car 7270 at Western and Bross in July 1950.
CERA Archives

Car 7227 at Western and Bross in October 1954. In this photo, we see a curve in the street pattern, which was unusual for Western Avenue.
William C. Hoffman Photo/Wien-Criss Archive

Car 7015 at Western and 34th in June 1956. The traffic warning sign at the right advised motorists to stop at the rear of streetcars, so as not to interfere with the loading and unloading of passengers.
William C. Hoffman Photo/Wien-Criss Archive

Car 7036 at Western and 35th in June 1956. This portion of Western and 35th Street presented a pleasant view with trees lining the street. Generations of Chicagoans knew that a white band on a black line pole indicated a car stop—no other identification was necessary.
Raymond DeGroote Photo

Car 7119 at Archer and Western on Christmas Eve 1953. The car is pulling off of Archer onto Western, for the trip to the Western-79th terminal.
Raymond DeGroote Photo

Car 7156 at Western and Archer in November 1954. The conductor is lifting the switch lever to allow the car to turn southwest onto Archer, where it would loop at Rockwell and 38th Street.
William C. Hoffman Photo/Wien-Criss Archive

Car 4406 at Western and Archer in August 1954. Three other PCCs line up on Western just north of Archer. The GM&O main line is in the distance. CTA's Orange Line began service in this area in 1993.
William C. Hoffman Photo/Wien-Criss Archive

A view of the unique "street car waiting room" located at Western and Archer, provided by the Czerwiec Lumber Company.
William C. Hoffman Photo/Wien-Criss Archive

Passengers are shown leaving the "street car waiting room" to board the approaching southbound Western Avenue "Green Hornet" in November 1954.
William C. Hoffman Photo/Wien-Criss Archive

Barely two months after streetcar service ended on Western, the "street car waiting" room was gutted by fire on August 20, 1956.
William C. Hoffman Photo/Wien-Criss Archive

Car 7236 at Archer and Western in November 1954, going under the Chicago Junction Railway overpass.
William C. Hoffman Photo/Wien-Criss Archive

Car 7208 at Western near Pershing Road in September 1950.
Truman D. Hefner Photo

Car 4017 on Western near 47th in May 1956.
William C. Janssen Photo/Krambles-Peterson Archive

Cars 4402 and 4407 pass each other at Western and 53rd in July 1950.
John E. Koschwanez Photo/Wien-Criss Archive

Car 4008 at Western and 65th in October 1955, running past a lineup of auto dealerships on Western.
William C. Hoffman Photo/Wien-Criss Archive

Car 4382 at Western and 66th in October 1953.
William C. Hoffman Photo/Wien-Criss Archive

Car 4060 at the same location two years later in October 1955.
William C. Hoffman Photo/Wien-Criss Archive

Western at 66th as it appeared in April 1957. The track has been paved over, the safety island removed, and new street lights installed. Overhead wire is still in place, ten months after the last streetcar ran in the area.
William C. Hoffman Photo/Wien-Criss Archive

Western at 66th in August 1957. By this time, the overhead wire had been removed.
William C. Hoffman Photo/Wien-Criss Archive

Western at 66th in May 1969. By now, the streetcars had been long gone, leaving no trace of their previous existence.
William C. Hoffman Photo/Wien-Criss Archive

Car 4015 at Western and 67th in June 1956. This is a view of what prospective riders saw every day- a streetcar approaching a safety island in traffic.
William C. Hoffman Photo/Wien-Criss Archive

Car 7157 at Western and 67th in June 1955. The PCCs, with their quick acceleration and braking, were more than an adequate match for competing traffic.
William C. Hoffman Photo/Wien-Criss Archive

Car 7123 at Western and 69th in January 1954. Car 7123 is a pull-out from the 69th Street Station (carbarn).
William C. Hoffman Photo/Wien-Criss Archive

Car 7193 at Western and 69th in October 1953 heads a lineup of "Green Hornets."
William C. Hoffman Photo/Wien-Criss Archive

Car 7164 at 69th Street Station in January 1954. The carbarn at 69th Street and Ashland was the South Side station for Western Avenue cars until September 5, 1954, when the cars were shifted over to the 77th Street Station at 77th and Vincennes. Streetcars were still running on Ashland at the time of this photo.
William C. Hoffman Photo/Wien-Criss Archive

Car 7203 at 69th Street Station in August 1953. This broadside shot reveals the pleasing lines of the St. Louis Car Company-built PCCs.
William C. Hoffman Photo/Wien-Criss Archive

Car 7240 at 69th and Morgan in October 1954. The car is shown as a pull-in to the 77th Street Station, after the closure of the 69th Street Station.
William C. Hoffman Photo/Wien-Criss Archive

Car 4056 at 69th and Emerald in May 1956. The car is running as a pull-in to the 79th Street Station.
William C. Janssen Photo/Krambles-Peterson Archive

Car 4375 at 69th and Hamilton in November 1954. Note the interesting lettering on the boxcar passing overhead, advertising the Delaware, Lackawanna & Western Railroad, the route of the "Phoebe Snow" passenger train, which ran between Hoboken, New Jersey, and Buffalo, New York.
William C. Hoffman Photo/Wien-Criss Archive

Car 4020 at Western and 71st in June 1956.
William C. Hoffman Photo/Wien-Criss Archive

Car 7042 at Western and 71st in June 1955. Track repairs on streetcar lines sometimes necessitated the use of a shoo-fly to divert cars around the track under repair.
William C. Hoffman Photo/Wien-Criss Archive

Car 7040 at Western and 73rd in July 1955. Car 7040 carefully negotiates its way over the temporary shoo-fly.
Richard C. Cerne Photo/CERA Archives

Car 7027 at Western and 73rd in July 1955. Two prewar cars, headed by 7027, await their turn over the shoo-fly.
Richard C. Cerne Photo/CERA Archives

Car 7004 at Western and 73rd in July 1955, taking its turn over the shoo-fly.
Richard C. Cerne Photo/CERA Archives

Car 4020 at Western and 73rd in June 1955, moving over the temporary installation, as a flagman is on hand to halt any northbound cars until clearance is received.
William C. Hoffman Photo/Wien-Criss Archive

Car 7031 at Western just north of 79th Street in May 1956.
William C. Janssen Photo/Krambles-Peterson Archive

Car 7154 at Western and 75th in March 1955. This photo was taken from the Wabash Railroad overpass.
Richard C. Cerne Photo/CERA Archives

Car 4010 entering the Western-79th Loop in November 1955.
Robert V. Mehlenbeck Photo/Krambles-Peterson Archive

Car 4373 at the Western-79th Loop in November 1952. In this view, we see two "Green Hornets" in Mercury Green, an ACF-Brill gas bus in Mercury Green, and another in Everglade Green.
William C. Hoffman Photo/Wien-Criss Archive

Car 7272 at the Western-79th Loop in May 1949. A motorman stands proudly in front of his new streamliner.
Robert W. Gibson Photo/Electric Railway Historical Society Collection

Car 7009 pulling out of the Western-79th Loop in November 1955, beginning is 15.6 mile journey to its northern terminal at Western-Berwyn.
Krambles-Peterson Archive

Postwar car 7256 and prewar PCC 4047 laying over at the Western-79th Loop.
Krambles-Peterson Archive

Car 7009 at the head of a lineup of five prewar PCCs at the Western-79th Loop in February 1956.
Krambles-Peterson Archive

Car 4016 at Western-79th Street Loop, in May 1956. This terminal loop looked very attractive with its neatly landscaped grounds.
William C. Janssen Photo/Krambles-Peterson Archive

Car 7037 at the Western-79th Loop in June 1956.
Raymond DeGroote Photo

63RD.
Ext.
AUG 3
W E
T C E S
STAMP HERE
SEE OTHER SIDE
TRANSFER NOT GOOD ON SURFACE DIVISION AFTER USING RAPID TRANSIT DIVISION UNLESS THE TIME IS STAMPED ON TRANSFER WHEN LEAVING RAPID TRANSIT STATION.
955174

HIMMEL
Lain
63 63-STONY ISLAND
64
4012

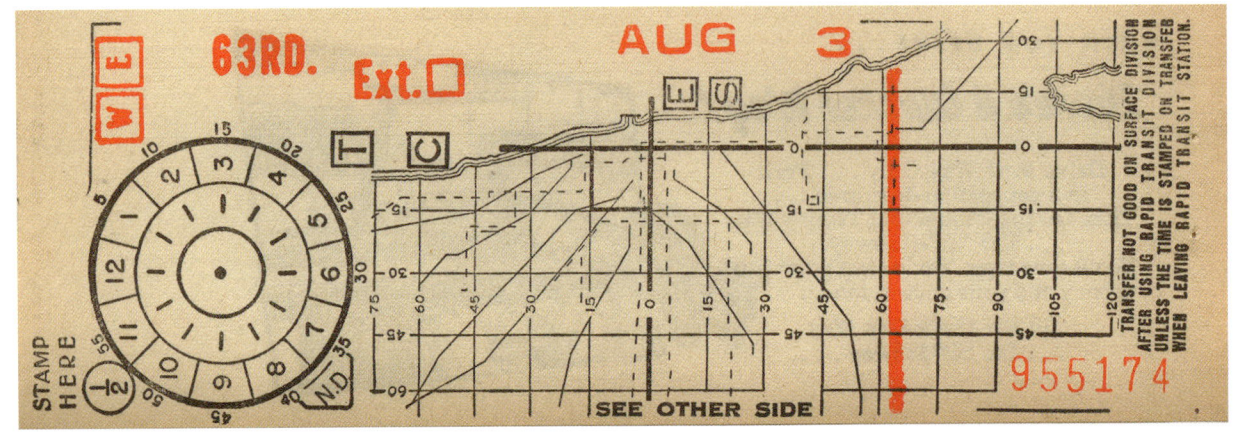

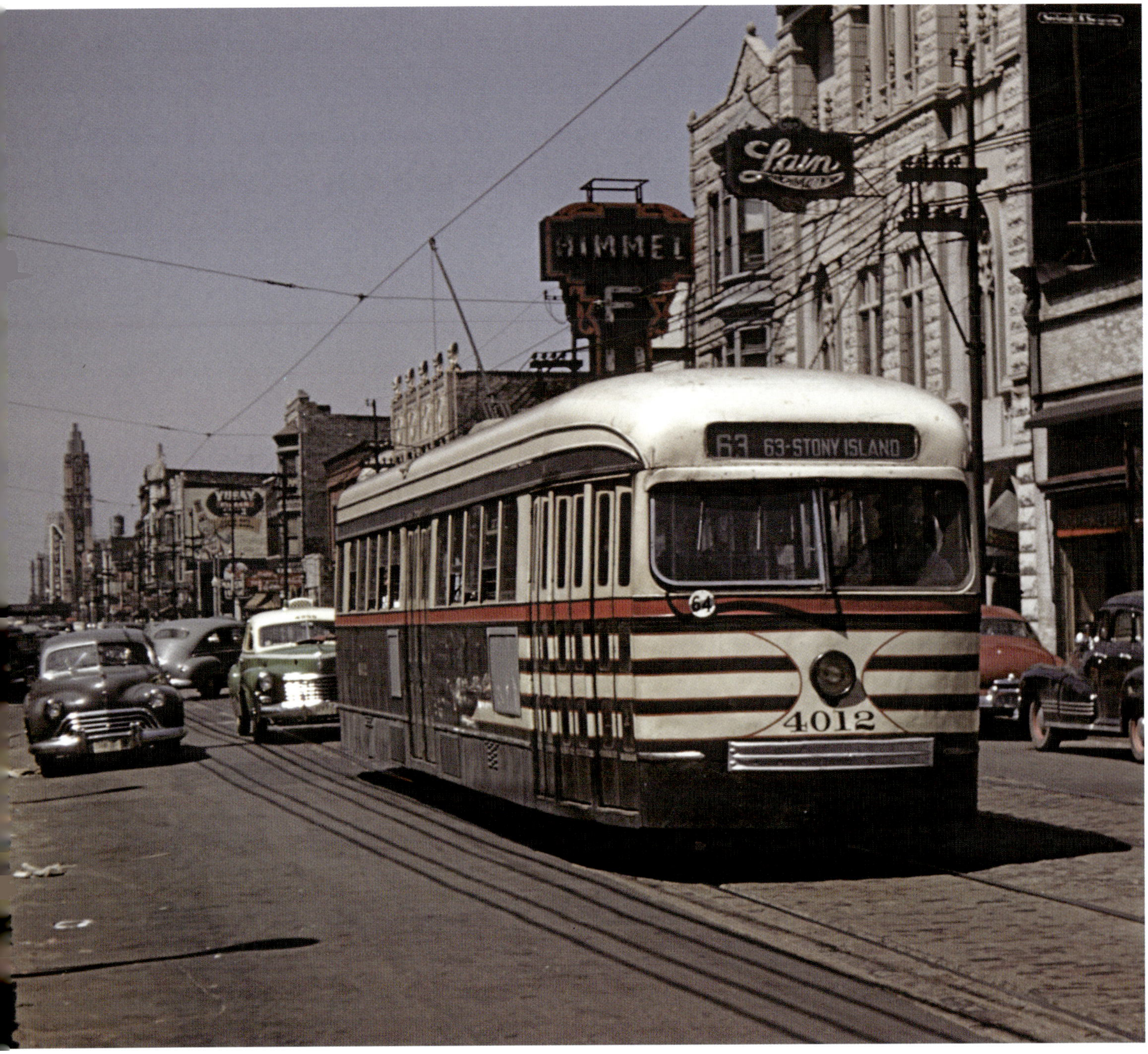

Route 63: 63rd

PCC Operations History

Spring 1948
Prewar PCCs gradually transferred from Madison St. to 63rd; assignment of prewar PCCs completed by June 1948.

January 1952
Prewar PCCs are gradually removed and replaced by standard red streetcars within a three-month period.

November 1952
Two-man postwar PCCs introduced to route to supplement standard red streetcars.

December 7, 1952
Buses substituted for streetcars on weekends.

May 23, 1953
PCCs and standard red streetcars replaced by buses.

Car 7019 pulling out of the turnback loop at 63rd Place and Narragansett in June 1949.
Robert W. Gibson Photo/Electric Railway Historical Society Collection

Cars 4015 and 4029, in contrasting CSL and CTA paint schemes, lay over at the 63rd Place-Narragansett Loop in April 1952.
Truman D. Hefner Photo

Car 7034, in CSL "tiger stripes," at the 63rd Place-Narragansett turnback loop in March 1952.
Gordon E. Lloyd Photo/John Bromley Collection

Car 4031 at 63rd Place and Narragansett, showing how sparsely populated the area was in November 1948.
George Krambles Photo/Krambles-Peterson Archive

Car 7005 on 63rd Place private right-of-way just east of Narragansett in September 1949. The Chicago system was not noted for having an abundance of such private right-of-way, but the westernmost mile of the 63rd Street line was a notable exception.
Truman D. Hefner Photo/John Bromley Collection

Car 7017 running eastbound on the 63rd Place private-right-of-way in March 1951, where the PCCs could keep up a quick pace.
Truman D. Heffner Photo/Krambles-Peterson Archive

Car 7022 zips through this snowy 1949 scene on 63rd Place, east of Narragansett.
Robert W. Gibson Photo/Electric Railway Historical Society Collection

Postwar car 7229 on 63rd Place east of Narragansett in February 1953.
William C. Janssen Photo/Krambles-Peterson Archive

Car 7023 on 63rd Place east of Narragansett in July 1950.
John E. Koschwanez Photo/John Bromley Collection

Car 4399 on 63rd Place at Menard, near the east end of the private right-of-way trackage, in February 1953.
William C. Janssen Photo/Krambles-Peterson Archive

Car 4037 on 63rd Place near Narragansett in this December 1952 winter scene.
Truman D. Hefner Photo

New construction is already apparent in the area around car 4019 on 63rd Place near Narragansett, in this December 1952 winter view.
Truman D. Hefner Photo

Car 4017 passes another PCC on 63rd Place near Narragansett in June 1951.
Truman D. Hefner Photo

Car 4010 on the 63rd Place private right-of-way in June 1951.
Truman D. Hefner Photo

Car 4004, just about to whiz by the photographer, on 63rd Place in June 1951.
Truman D. Hefner Photo

Car 4019 on the 63rd Place private right-of-way in September 1949.
Krambles-Peterson Archive

Car 4009 near 63rd Place and Central, just east of the private right-of-way section, in June 1951.
Henry Stange Jr. Photo/Krambles-Peterson Archive

Car 4020 emerges from a wye at 63rd Place and Central Avenue in June 1951.
Truman D. Hefner Photo

Car 4021, the only prewar car saved, heads east near 63rd and Lindner in May 1951. Midway Airport, then the world's busiest, is at left.
William C. Hoffman Photo/Wien-Criss Archive

On December 18, 1949, a TWA L-049 overshot the runway while landing and ended up in the street at 63rd and Cicero. Safety procedures were different than they are today. Trolley service continued, in spite of the fire risk from airplane fuel on the street. The next day's *Chicago Tribune* reported, "Had the plane continued into 63rd Street, it probably would have hit high power trolley wires."
CERA Archives

Car 4013 at a grade crossing near 63rd and Kilbourn in June 1951.
Truman D. Hefner Photo/John Bromley Collection

Car 4027 on 63rd and Central Park, after emerging from the Grand Trunk Western underpass, in June 1951. The car at right either has an unusual two-tone color scheme, or has a fender from a junk yard.
Henry Stange Jr. Photo/Krambles-Peterson Archive

Car 4027 on 63rd near Central Park in June 1951.
Henry Stange Jr. Photo/Krambles-Peterson Archive

Car 4027 is westbound on 63rd near Central Park in June 1951.
George Krambles Photo/Krambles-Peterson Archive

PCC car 7020 passes red Pullman 278 in this June 1951 view from the Grand Trunk Western embankment.
Robert W. Gibson Photo/Electric Railway Historical Society Collection

Car 7248 emerges from the 63rd-Central Park wye in March 1950, ready to head east.
Krambles-Peterson Archive

Car 7002, pulling out of the wye at 63rd and Central Park in June 1951.
George Krambles Photo/Krambles-Peterson Archive

Car 7002, at 63rd and Central Park, avoids local kids riding bicycles in June 1951.
George Krambles Photo/Krambles-Peterson Archive

A good view of the rear of car 7002, as it heads east on 63rd and Central Park in June 1951. One of those little neighborhood stores, so typical of Chicago in the 1950s, is at left.
George Krambles Photo/Krambles-Peterson Archive

Car 7016 paces a late 1940s Cadillac on 63rd near Maplewood in May 1951.
William C. Hoffman Photo/Wien-Criss Archive

Car 7011, still in CSL "tiger stripes," stops to pick up and discharge passengers on 63rd and Western in June 1950.
William C. Hoffman Photo/Wien-Criss Archive

Car 7032 eastbound at 63rd and Lowe in May 1949. The Southtown Theater, an Englewood landmark with 3,202 seats, is visible down the street. It closed in August 1958, and was torn down in 1991.
CERA Archives

Cars 638 and 4377, the old and the new, pass each other on 63rd Street and Harvard in this December 1952 view. *Truman D. Hefner Photo*

Much the same view as the previous picture, but taken in April 1986. In 34 years, the cityscape had radically changed, with many of the buildings in the earlier photo being bulldozed, leaving empty lots in their wake. The former Southtown Theater had not yet been demolished.
Jeffrey L. Wien Photo/Wien-Criss Archive

Car 4012 heads east on 63rd and Harvard in August 1950.
Henry Stange Jr. Photo/Krambles-Peterson Archive

Car 7030, heading westbound on 63rd near State, offering a good view of the old Englewood Union Station as it looked in 1950. At one time, you could catch trains from the Rock Island, Nickel Plate, New York Central, and Pennsylvania Railroad here.
John R. Williams Photo/Krambles-Peterson Archive

Car 4028 in July 1950, offering a closer view of a prewar PCC at the same Englewood Union Station location as the previous picture.
Robert W. Gibson Photo/Electric Railway Historical Society Collection

Car 4038 is eastbound on 63rd near Wabash in March 1952.
Truman D. Hefner Photo

Car 4409 under the Jackson Park "L" on 63rd at Blackstone in February 1953.
William C. Janssen Photo/Krambles-Peterson Archive

Car 4037, under the 63rd Street "L" near Stony Island, passes a Woolworth's dime store in December 1952. *Truman D. Hefner Photo*

Car 4013 has just turned from 63rd onto Stony Island, as it prepares to go around the block and head back west in November 1951. This was the eastern end of the Jackson Park "L" at the time, but this branch has since been cut back to Cottage Grove. Part of the Greyhound Bus Terminal is visible at left.
Truman D. Hefner Photo

Car 4032 Stony Island in 1949, at much the same location as the previous picture. Here we see the unusual "dogleg" in the streetcar tracks.
CERA Archives

Car 7009 making the turn at 63rd and Stony Island in 1951. That may be a 1950 Ford to the right of the streetcar.
John E. Koschwanez Photo/John Bromley Collection

Car 4373 prepares to make the turn from Stony Island onto 64th in February 1953. A red Pullman is just barely visible at left.
William C. Janssen Photo/Krambles-Peterson Archive

Car 7273 joins the lineup of PCCs and red cars on 64th as it turns the corner from Stony Island in February 1953.
William C. Janssen Photo/Krambles-Peterson Archive

Car 4023 laying over at the end of the line on 64th just west of Stony Island in July 1951. This car is going to short turn at Central Park.
William C. Hoffman Photo/Wien-Criss Archive

Car 4029 at the end of the line near Jackson Park, on 64th west of Stony Island in March 1952.
Truman D. Hefner Photo

The Last Chicago Streetcar

By mid-1954, with the elimination of the last of the red streetcar lines, Chicago found itself with just four streetcar lines: Broadway/State, Clark/Wentworth, Cottage Grove, and Western, all of them equipped with PCC cars. It wasn't long before three of these lines were replaced with buses and with the run of the last car on the Broadway/Downtown line in the early morning of February 16, 1957, Chicago was down to just one streetcar line--Clark/Wentworth.

The route would not remain intact throughout 1957, however, as the northern portion of the line (with the heaviest traffic) from Clark and Kinzie to Clark and Howard, was converted to bus in the early hours of September 7, 1957. All that remained was the Wentworth portion running from Clark and Kinzie to a wye at 81st and Halsted. The handwriting was definitely on the wall and everyone waited for the announced conversion date of Chicago's last streetcar line.

The CTA and the City of Chicago soon found themselves with a perfect opportunity to quietly bring down the curtain on almost a century of streetcar operation in Chicago. The new Congress "L" line running in the median strip of the Congress Street expressway was due to be opened on Sunday, June 22, 1958. Both Mayor Daley and the media would be on hand to welcome in a new era in Chicago transportation. The last of an "old era"—the last streetcar line—was then slated to be converted to bus early on Saturday morning, June 21. By the arrangements of these dates, it seemed the powers that be hoped to usher the new era in with a bang and let the other die with a whimper.

Thus it was that PCC car 7213 edged its way out of the wye at 81st and Halsted on June 21 at 4:15 a.m. to begin its last round trip over the line. The differences could not have been greater for the crew assigned to the last run. Motorman Marvin McFall had begun his career with the predecessor Chicago Surface Lines in 1926 and had been operating streetcars over the Clark/Wentworth route for the past 32 years. He had always selected night runs out of the Devon terminal and later (after the Clark St. portion closed) out of 77th and Vincennes. Conductor William Rye, on the other hand, could hardly have felt nostalgic about making this last trip as he had only been with CTA since April 21, just two months earlier.

The car was crammed with streetcar enthusiasts who lustily cheered any remaining southbound PCCs that passed them while roundly booing the replacement buses they encountered. Red crepe paper (the fans couldn't find any in black) and hand-painted signs were attached to the car to advertise to all that this was, as the crudely lettered sign on the front of the car boldly stated, the "LAST STREETCar to run in Chicago."

Ronald J. Johnson Photo/Wien-Criss Archive

Ronald J. Johnson Photo/Wien-Criss Archive

Opposite: The last motorman Marvin McFall and conductor William Rye shake hands at the end of the final run. *CTA Historical Collection*

Car 7213 on Halsted and 81st on the final run.
D. Greer Nielsen Photo/Wien-Criss Archive

Car 7213 on Halsted and 81st following the final run. Fans were then allowed to ride with the car to the carbarn, but they all had to get off first.
William C. Hoffman Photo/Wien-Criss Archive

Fans have now reboarded car 7213 for one last time as it prepares to head to the barn.
William C. Hoffman Photo/Wien-Criss Archive

When 7213 turned onto Kinzie from Dearborn and readied itself for the final leg of the journey into transit history, photographers from the Chicago newspapers were on hand to record the event. While motorman McFall waved farewell to a photographer from the *Sun-Times,* others on hand were making preparations to ensure that the last run did indeed go out with a BANG. As 7213 turned south onto Clark Street, several torpedoes placed on the rail heads detonated with a series of loud cracks. A couple of passengers thought they were hearing gun shots, but almost everyone else knew the real cause of the commotion.

Chicago's last streetcar at 81st and Halsted, at the south end of the line following the final run.
Robert W. Gibson Photo/Electric Railway Historical Society Collection

There were no more PCCs to pass as 7213 effortlessly glided along its southbound route, only the propane buses CTA had selected to replace the streetcars. Dawn had broken by the time the car wyed at 81st and Halsted terminal and then began its pull-in run to the South Shops with everyone still on board where it arrived around 6:00 a.m.

At the South Shops fans gathered around to take their final photos of the streetcar. For many it was hard to say good-bye to a cherished institution that had been such an important part of the daily lives of countless Chicagoans. The 7213 pulled up in front of the barn for the last time as part of a row of streetcars that would never again be called to duty.

Out of 600 postwar PCC streetcars, only one remains in operation today. Car 4391 can still be ridden at the Illinois Railway Museum and serve as a reminder to Chicagoans of the swift, clean, electric surface transportation we once enjoyed and which is now lost forever.

Lineup on completion of last runs at 78th and Vincennes. Notice car 4391, the third-to-last operated.
CTA Historical Collection

Preserved Chicago PCC Cars

The 4021 Story

When the Western Avenue car line was converted to motor buses on June 17, 1956, the CTA retired all of the remaining 1936 PCC cars. At that time they were authorized to be scrapped, but one car, 4021, was supposedly going to be sold to a private individual. Apparently this sale fell through, but CTA decided to retain the car and add it to the collection of historic streetcars assembled over a period of years by Chicago Surface Lines, which were stored at the 77th Street station.

After the end of streetcar service on June 21, 1958, car 4021 and other historic streetcars were moved to a former carbarn located at Lincoln and Wrightwood and later to another at Cermak and Lawndale. Over the years various CTA managements considered putting the historic streetcars on public display, but nothing ever resulted from the various proposals. Finally in 1984, the CTA donated most of the historic streetcar collection, including car 4021, to the Illinois Railway Museum in Union, Illinois. The car was cosmetically restored to its 1936 appearance where it is on public display as a static vehicle.

Front and rear views of car 4021, freshly repainted at the Illinois Railway Museum, in June 2009.
Frank Hicks Photo

Car 4391 at Vincennes and 78th in June 1958.
Robert D. Heinlein Photo

Car 4391 at Wentworth and 40th on Route 22 in June 1958.
Charles L. Tauscher Photo/Wien-Criss Archive

The interior of car 4021, as it looked in June 1999 at the Illinois Railway Museum.
John Marton Photo

The 4391 Story

Ordered by the Chicago Surface Lines (Chicago Railways Company) in January 1946, PCC car 4391 was delivered to the Chicago Transit Authority on June 9, 1948. Car 4391 was placed in revenue service on June 15, 1948, and was retired from service on June 21, 1958 (ten years and one week later). The car was sold to the Electric Railway Historical Society (ERHS) in June 1959 and was moved to the group's carbarn located in suburban Downers Grove in November 1959. The car remained on static display in Downers Grove until May 1973 when it was moved to the Illinois Railway Museum in Union, Illinois. Upon its arrival at IRM, work was begun to restore the car to operating condition. The fruit of that labor was realized on June 22, 1975, when the 4391 operated again for the first time in 17 years. It has been regularly operating in revenue service at the museum since late 1976.

During its ten-year career plying the streets of Chicago, car 4391, commonly called a "Green Hornet," operated primarily on routes 22–Clark/Wentworth, 36–Broadway/State, 49–Western, 63–63rd Street, and occasionally on 8–Halsted and 42–Halsted/Downtown. The "MUSEUM" destination sign was used for Route 22–Clark Street cars that operated during the late 1940s and early 1950s between Clark/Howard and the Field Museum loop at Roosevelt and Lake Shore Drive. Green Hornet 4391 operated on the last day of streetcar service in Chicago—June 21, 1958. During its entire career it was operated as a two-man car. As such, passengers entered at the rear and exited via the center and front doors.

Between February 1954 and August 1958, 570 of the original fleet of 600 Green Hornet streetcars were shipped to St. Louis Car Company where component parts such as door motors, traction motors, trucks, windows, and seats were used in the construction of CTA rapid transit cars numbered 6201-6720 and 1-50. Of the 30 remaining Green Hornets not used in the construction of rapid transit cars, 29 were scrapped. Of the original fleet of 600 Green Hornet streetcars, only car 4391 survives to this day.

Car 4391 on Vincennes at 76th in June 1958.
Robert D. Heinlein Photo

Car 4391 on Western at Winnebago in June 1950.
Krambles-Peterson Archive

The Story of the Acquisiton of CTA PCC 4391
by Frank Hicks

At the time the 4391 was sold, Glenn Anderson was an engineering assistant in the Staff Engineer's office at CTA. His background in PCC cars (surface and rapid transit) was as an instructor in the school at the former Division car barn where maintenance employees were trained. Much of the work was to update the skills of the older men who were familiar only with 4000s, wooden rapid transit cars, or pre-PCC streetcars.

Simultaneously, Glenn was part of the Electric Railway Historical Society, which had several older streetcars stored on rented farmland south of Downers Grove.

Also at that time back in Chicago, the last of the 600 Green Hornets (postwar PCC streetcars) were winding down. A few had been wrecked in service, one had gone to Pullman and one to St. Louis Car Company for examination as to whether the bodies could be reworked as rapid transit cars. By then 570 had been shipped to the St. Louis Car Company for salvage of components to be used with entirely new body shells as rapid transit cars 6201-6720 and 1-50; that left 27 of the Green Hornets stored at the South Shops.

CTA offered for sale a group of 18 cars believed to be in operating condition and 2 cars not in operating condition; bids were invited on all or part of these 20 cars. For the price which a buyer offered, the shop would load the car on a railroad flat car and secure it ready for shipment via the track connection to the Belt Railway of Chicago.

The ERHS wanted to purchase one of the cars and Glenn could assess which one would be the most promising. First he looked at the maintenance record and that ruled out about half of the 18 cars as suitable candidates. Then he went under each of the cars where they stood "on the flat" (not over inspection pits) in the yard at the South Shops, dropped the equipment covers and checked to see that all of the components were intact and in good condition. His inspection ruled out some more cars, such as if an electrical fire had burned out any of the equipment compartments. The result: the 4391 was the best available car.

ERHS did not have railroad access, but preferred shipment by truck as had been done with the cars already at Downers Grove. ERHS used Helders, a heavy machinery trucking service on 26th Street. They didn't normally handle rail cars but could do it with assistance from Bill McGregor of ERHS. Bill was a practical man who could determine how to lift, load and secure streetcars, even by use of jacks without any cranes if necessary. Therefore, there would be no need for the shops to load the car for ERHS. Glenn found out how many man-hours it took when the shops loaded one so they could judge the basis by which an ERHS bid for a car on its own wheels would be compared with anyone else's bid for a car aboard a flat car.

When bids were submitted, the two high bids were ERHS's bid for car 4391 and a bid by a dealer for all of the cars (which included 4391). The dealer hoped to resell the 18 operable cars for operation in Mexico City. His bid was higher (after adjustment for loading the car) by ONE DOLLAR per car!

Glenn went to see Miss Benson, the administrative assistant to Mr. Graybiel. The latter was the store room foreman in charge of Store Room 50, the section responsible for scrap sales which had received the bids on behalf of CTA. Sadly, Miss Benson told Glenn she couldn't do anything for him. The dealer's bid was higher even though by only a dollar and the rules of the game were that the high bidder wins. However, she told Glenn who the high bidder was and suggested that he contact the winner.

Glenn phoned the dealer and had a constructive conversation with him. Glenn cautioned him that the Chicago cars were probably too large to fit the clearances in Mexico City, which the man

Car 4391 in 78th Street Yard, awaiting final disposition on June 26, 1959, more than a year after the end of service.
Jeffrey L. Wien Photo/Wien-Criss Archive

Car 4391 on November 2, 1959, loaded on a trailer for its trip to Downers Grove, after being purchased by the Electric Railway Historical Society. It is appropriately signed "Museum."
Jeffrey L. Wien Photo/Wien-Criss Archive

apparently hadn't considered. The dealer said he would get back to Glenn if the Mexico City deal fell through.

After six months Glenn called the dealer again. It turned out he was right about the size of the cars, which didn't hurt his standing with the dealer! But the fellow had another idea for sale, this time components. Again he said he would get back to Glenn if he couldn't make the sale.

Another six months elapsed and the cars were clearly visible to any passerby along 79th Street. Glenn dropped into Miss Benson's office, She said that CTA was about to remind the dealer to remove his cars from CTA property.

Before Glenn could reach the dealer, however, the dealer phoned Glenn. He did indeed need all 20 cars for components to be resold to a customer of his in Belgium. But the rest of the cars didn't matter for that purpose; he was going to scrap them (which eventually was done at 67th Street and Cicero Avenue by Merchants Steel and Supply Company). So he proposed a trade to Glenn. If ERHS could buy another wrecked car, one not in the group of 20 which CTA had offered, it could be an even-Steven trade. ERHS could have the 4391 and Belgium could have the components from that twenty-first car. It turned out to be another St. Louis-built car, 7218.

Meanwhile, back to Miss Benson. There was another car that was never on the bid list. Could ERHS buy it? She said she'd talk to Graybiel adding "I'm sure he'll let you have it for the price of the others, less the loading cost."

So the deal was made. Bob Selle at ERHS very much wanted the car and did some quick and ambitious fund raising. Glen paid a little more than half of the price out-of-pocket as a contribution to ERHS. The ERHS treasury (whose revenue stream was publication of historical books) paid approximately the shipping cost. Bill McGregor got the body onto a Helders trailer.

Unlike a conventional car, taking a fully skirted PCC off the trucks saved only a few inches in height. Bill McGregor had the dimensions figured out so that it would fit the highway clearances provided that it was loaded backwards to fit better around the gooseneck of the trailer. They had to remove the trolley shroud, base, and hook from the roof. Off went the car to Downers Grove and soon it was unloaded there.

One reason why the 4391 (or some others) was a good selection was a byproduct of its assignment over the few years of its operational life. It was a pure two-man car; it hadn't been retrofitted for part- or full-time one-man operation as some had. Much of the time it had been assigned to 69th Street station which supplied half of the cars for the 49-Western line. That was a long line, but it didn't have the extremely heavy loads for much of the day and night the way Clark Street did. However, Western Avenue at that time was operated on weekends with one-man buses, and 69th had plenty of indoor storage space. Even after Western was made one-man in 1955, the 4391 was over at 77th station because it could no longer be used on Western, so again it was indoors all weekend. Therefore, it was a fairly low-mileage car and had been well protected from the elements. Had it been at Devon, where more than half of the storage was outdoors, it would not have been as desirable.

Like all of the Green Hornets, the car had been delivered in Mercury (or Colorado Spruce) green with a Swamp Holly orange belt. Like some others, this one had been brush-painted at South Shops in the new darker Everglade green which covered the Mercury green and Swamp Holly orange on the lower sides, belt, and the band though the standee windows. Because the Croydon cream top was in fairly good condition, it came to ERHS with this original paint still there.

Another view of car 4391 on November 2, 1959, ready to leave CTA property.
Jeffrey L. Wien Photo/Wien-Criss Archive

It was a cold and snowy winter day when car 4391 departed 78th and Vincennes for good.
Jeffrey L. Wien Photo/Wien-Criss Archive

It also had most of the original leather seat covers; others had been replaced with vinyl due to cuts or other damage. Bob Gibson and Bill McGregor went out to South Shops and swapped out the vinyl seat backs and bottom cushions into other cars, finding enough leather ones to make up a full set for 4391.

The roof paint—original, remember, in the days before a coat of paint was expected to last decades—had failed in large splotches not visible from the ground. The fellows at ERHS initially took care of that with red lead.

Eventually the farm at Downers Grove was to be redeveloped (you wouldn't recognize the spot today) and the cars had to be moved. That was when Helders moved them again, this time from Downers Grove to the Illinois Railway Museum at Union. Frank Sirinek and the other folks there subsequently repainted the entire car in the original livery, adding a new coat of Croydon cream for the upper body and roof. The IRM duty cycle is even less demanding than on Western Avenue, so it is indoors much more than just two days a week and the paint should last a long time.

Car 4391 as it appeared on November 2, 1959, having just arrived at the ERHS farm in Downers Grove. *Jeffrey L. Wien Photo/Wien-Criss Archive*

Car 4391 in Downers Grove in 1968, ten years after the end of service.
Jeffrey L. Wien Photo/Wien-Criss Archive

Car 4391 at the ERHS barn in Downers Grove in June 1968.
Jeffrey L. Wien Photo/Wien-Criss Archive

Frank Sirinek (left) and Steve Iversen working on one of 4391's trucks at the Illinois Railway Museum in October 1974.
Jeffrey L. Wien Photo/Wien-Criss Archive

Car 4391, being repainted into CSL colors, in May 1975.
Jeffrey L. Wien Photo/Wien-Criss Archive

Car 4391, looking magnificent in its new paint scheme in May 1975.
Jeffrey L. Wien Photo/Wien-Criss Archive

Car 4391, newly repainted at IRM in May 1975.
Jeffrey L. Wien Photo/Wien-Criss Archive

A full-length view of 4391 at IRM in May 1975.
Jeffrey L. Wien Photo/Wien-Criss Archive

Car 4391 on its first day of operation at IRM, June 22, 1975, just over 17 years since it last ran in Chicago.
Jeffrey L. Wien Photo/Wien-Criss Archive

Motorman Frank Sirinek is ready to take car 4391 around the trolley loop in this 1976 photo.
Jeffrey L. Wien Photo/Wien-Criss Archive

Bob Gibson, who helped both to document and save car 4391 for posterity, poses in front of the car when it was brought back to Daley Plaza in October 1987 to help mark the 40th anniversary of CTA.
Robert W. Gibson Photo/Electric Railway Historical Society Collection

Car 4391 on display in Daley plaza in October 1987.
Jeffrey L. Wien Photo/Wien-Criss Archive

Another view of 4391 in Daley Plaza in October 1987.
Jeffrey L. Wien Photo/Wien-Criss Archive

Car 4406 on State at 34th in October 1955, offering a fine view of a "Safety Island." This photo was used in order to make the Illinois Railway Museum's reproduction Safety Island.
William C. Hoffman Photo/Wien-Criss Archive

Car 4391 stops at a reproduction Safety Island at IRM in August 2000.
Jeffrey L. Wien Photo/Wien-Criss Archive

Car 4391 poses with CTA trolley coach 9631 at IRM in 1985.
David Sadowski Photo

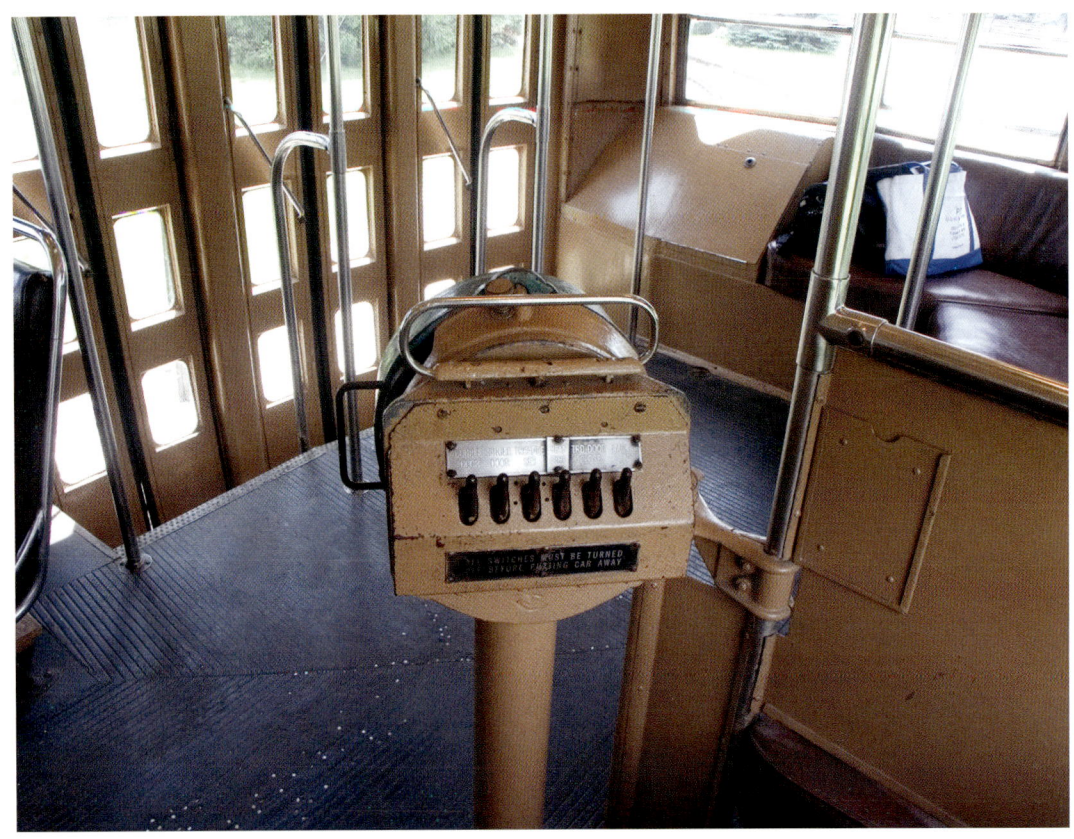
Car 4391 interior showing conductor's fare register device, June 2008.
Bradley Criss Photo/Wien-Criss Archive

Car 4391 interior, showing rear doors, in June 2008.
Bradley Criss Photo/Wien-Criss Archive

Car 4391 interior, June 2008.
Bradley Criss Photo/Wien-Criss Archive

Frank Sirinek at the controls of 4391 in July 1985.
David Sadowski Photo

The motorman's position in car 4391 in July 1985.
David Sadowski Photo

Car 4391 interior, June 2008.
Bradley Criss Photo/Wien-Criss Archive

Car 4391 interior showing conductor's position in June 2008.
Bradley Criss Photo/Wien-Criss Archive

Car 4391 interior showing close-up of conductor's fare register device, June 2008.
Bradley Criss Photo/Wien-Criss Archive

Car 4391 interior, showing motorman's controls and gauges, in June 2008.
Bradley Criss Photo/Wien-Criss Archive

Car 4391 interior with leather seats, June 2008.
Bradley Criss Photo/Wien-Criss Archive

Car 4391 interior, showing the St. Louis Car Co. builder's plate, in June 2008.
Bradley Criss Photo/Wien-Criss Archive

Car 4399 at 77th St. Yards in August 1959.
Jeffrey L. Wien Photo/Wien-Criss Archive

Cars 7218, 4378, and 4399 in 77th St. Yards, August 1959.
Jeffrey L. Wien Photo/Wien-Criss Archive

Cars 4399, 4378, and 7218 in 77th St. Yards in August 1959.
Jeffrey L. Wien Photo/Wien-Criss Archive

Cars 4407 and 4409 at 67th and Cicero in June 1959.
Jeffrey L. Wien Photo/Wien-Criss Archive

Car 4408 at 67th and Cicero in June 1959.
Jeffrey L. Wien Photo/Wien-Criss Archive

Car 4396 at 67th and Cicero in June 1959.
Jeffrey L. Wien Photo/Wien-Criss Archive

Cars 4407 and 4409 at 67th and Cicero in June 1959.
Jeffrey L. Wien Photo/Wien-Criss Archive

Tribute PCCs in Kenosha and San Francisco

While only two Chicago PCCs were preserved intact, and only one is operational, two other cities (San Francisco and Kenosha) have paid tribute to Chicago by painting their cars in our color schemes. Chicago's 683 PCC streetcars had unique characteristics, being longer than standard cars, and used a third set of doors for two-man operation. The tribute PCCs are therefore not exact replicas, but utilize standard one-man cars built during the same general era for other cities.

As of this writing, both tribute cars are operational and are used in regular service.

Kenosha

Kenosha Area Transit began operating a modern tourist trolley in June 2000, using cars originally built for Toronto. According to the Wikipedia:

> Kenosha's five historic 'Red Rocket' PCC A15-class streetcars were built in Fort William, Ontario (now part of Thunder Bay, Ontario) for the Toronto Transportation Commission (predecessor of the current Toronto Transit Commission) in 1951 by Canadian Car and Foundry Company under license from the Transit Research Corporation, holder of the PCC Car patents, and using car bodies manufactured by the St. Louis Car Company that were shipped to Canada, and were remanufactured and rebodied from the windows down in 1991.

Kenosha's car 4606 has been designated as the "Chicago car," and wears the same classic CSL colors as San Francisco's. It has the further distinction of riding on authentic Chicago PCC trucks, which were salvaged from 6000-series Chicago rapid transit cars. These, in turn, used recycled parts from 570 of Chicago's 600 postwar PCCs. Therefore, the Kenosha car is as close to being an authentic Chicago PCC as it is possible to get, using available cars and components made during the 1936-52 PCC era.

San Francisco

San Francisco's Municipal Railway operates a diverse fleet of historic streetcars and has designated 1058 as the "Chicago car." This car was originally built by St. Louis Car Co. in 1948 for the Philadelphia Transportation Company as No. 2124. Muni purchased it from SEPTA, the successor agency, in 1992. The car was repainted in 1995 with the opening of Muni's F-line. Originally in CTA colors—Everglade Green and Cream—Car 1058 was given a makeover in 2010 with Mercury Green, Croydon Cream, and Swamp Holly Orange, the 1946 CSL paint scheme.

Opposite: Kenosha car 4606 at 54th Street and 1st Avenue in December 2006. *Jeffrey L. Wien Photo/Wien-Criss Archive*

Kenosha car 4606 at 54th Street and 8th Avenue in December 2006.
Jeffrey L. Wien Photo/Wien-Criss Archive

Kenosha car 4606 at 54th Street and 7th Avenue in December 2006.
Jeffrey L. Wien Photo/Wien-Criss Archive

SF Muni Car 1058 on Don Chee Way turning onto the Embarcadero in May 2013.
Jeffrey L. Wien Photo/Wien-Criss Archive

SF Muni Car 1058 on the Embarcadero, turning into Don Chee Way in May 2013.
Jeffrey L. Wien Photo/Wien-Criss Archive

SF Muni Car 1058 on Market, turning into Noe in May 2013.
Jeffrey L. Wien Photo/Wien-Criss Archive

Car 4391 at the Illinois Railway Museum in July 1983.
David Sadowski Photo

Chicago PCC Roster

Numbers	Total Cars	Owner	Builder	Date	Seats	Length	Width	Height	Weight	Trucks	Motors	Remarks
4001	1	CRY	Pullman	1934	58	50' 5"	97"	10' 6 9/16"	36,000	Christensen	4-W1430D	Pullman sample pre-PCC car
7001	1	CCRY	Brill	1934	58	49' 0"	98"	10' 1/2"	37,200	B-95E	4-GE1178A1	Brill sample pre-PCC car
4002-4051	50	CRY	St. Louis	1936	58	50' 5"	104"	10' 1/8"	36,400	Clark B-2	4-WH1432	Car 4021 preserved at Illinois Railway Museum
7002-7034	33	CCRY	St. Louis	1936	58	50' 5"	104"	10' 1/8"	35,780	Clark B-2	4-GE-1198	
4052-4061	10	CRY	St. Louis	1947	57	50' 0"	108"	10' 3"	39,800	St. Louis B-3	4-WH1432	
7035-7114	80	CCRY	St. Louis	1947	57	50' 0"	108"	10' 3"	39,800	St. Louis B-3	4-WH1432	Car 7078 burned in collision May 1950
4062-4171	110	CRY	Pullman	1947	57	50' 0"	108"	10' 3"	42,000	Clark B-2	4-GE1220	
4172-4371	200	CRY	Pullman	1948	57	50' 0"	108"	10' 3"	42,000	Clark B-2	4-GE1220	
4372-4411	40	CRY	St. Louis	1948	57	50' 0"	108"	10' 3"	39,800	St. Louis B-3	4-WH1432	Car 4391 Preserved at Illinois Railway Museum
7115-7274	160	CCRY	St. Louis	1948	57	50' 0"	108"	10' 3"	39,800	St. Louis B-3	4-WH1432	

Chicago PCC Trivia

Chicago Railways Company, Owner of Cars 4002-4171
Chicago City Railway Company, Owner of Cars 7002-7224
All cars owned by Chicago Transit Authority as of October 1, 1947

Cars 4002-4051 were converted to one-man operation April-May 1952. Fare collection changed from Pay as You Pass to Pay as You Enter. Nos. 4032 and 7026 equipped with forced air ventilation.

Nos. 4052-4053, 4055-4058, 7035-7036, 7040, 7044, 7049, 7052-7053, 7057-7058, 7060, 7062, 7064, 7067-7068, 7070-7071, 7074 (24 cars) converted for one-man operation May 1952.

Nos. 4054, 4059, 4061, 7037-7039, 7041-7043 (9 cars) converted for one-man operation June 1955.

No. 7078 burned in collision with gasoline truck on May 25, 1950.

Nos. 7235-7259 (25 cars) converted to one-man operation June 1955.

Nos. 4052-4377, 4379, 4381-4386, 7035-7044, 7086-7216, 7219-7274 (570 cars) sold to St. Louis Car Company between 1953 and 1958. Salvaged components were used in the construction of PCC "L" cars 6201-6720 and 1-50.

Chicago PCC Facts: First two-man PCCs constructed; only PCCs equipped with a foot gong; largest fleet of PCC cars purchased new; the longest single-ended PCCs; the only PCCs equipped with hand controls (two-man operation); the only PCCs equipped with three sets of doors.

By the end of 1948, all 600 new PCC cars had been accepted for delivery and placed into service. The assignments of the new cars were as follows:
    20-Madison: 100 Pullman-built PCCs
    49-Western: 100 St. Louis-built PCCs
    22-Clark-Wentworth and 36-Broadway-State: 400 Pullman and St. Louis-built PCCs
    63-63rd Street: 83 prewar PCCs reassigned from 20-Madison in 1948.

The carbarn assignments at the end of 1948 were:
    Clark-Devon: Routes 22, 36, 49
    77th & Vincennes: Routes 22, 36
    Ashland-69th: Routes: 49, 63
    Kedzie-Van Buren: Route 20
    Also, a few cars at Cottage-38th

1936 PCCs

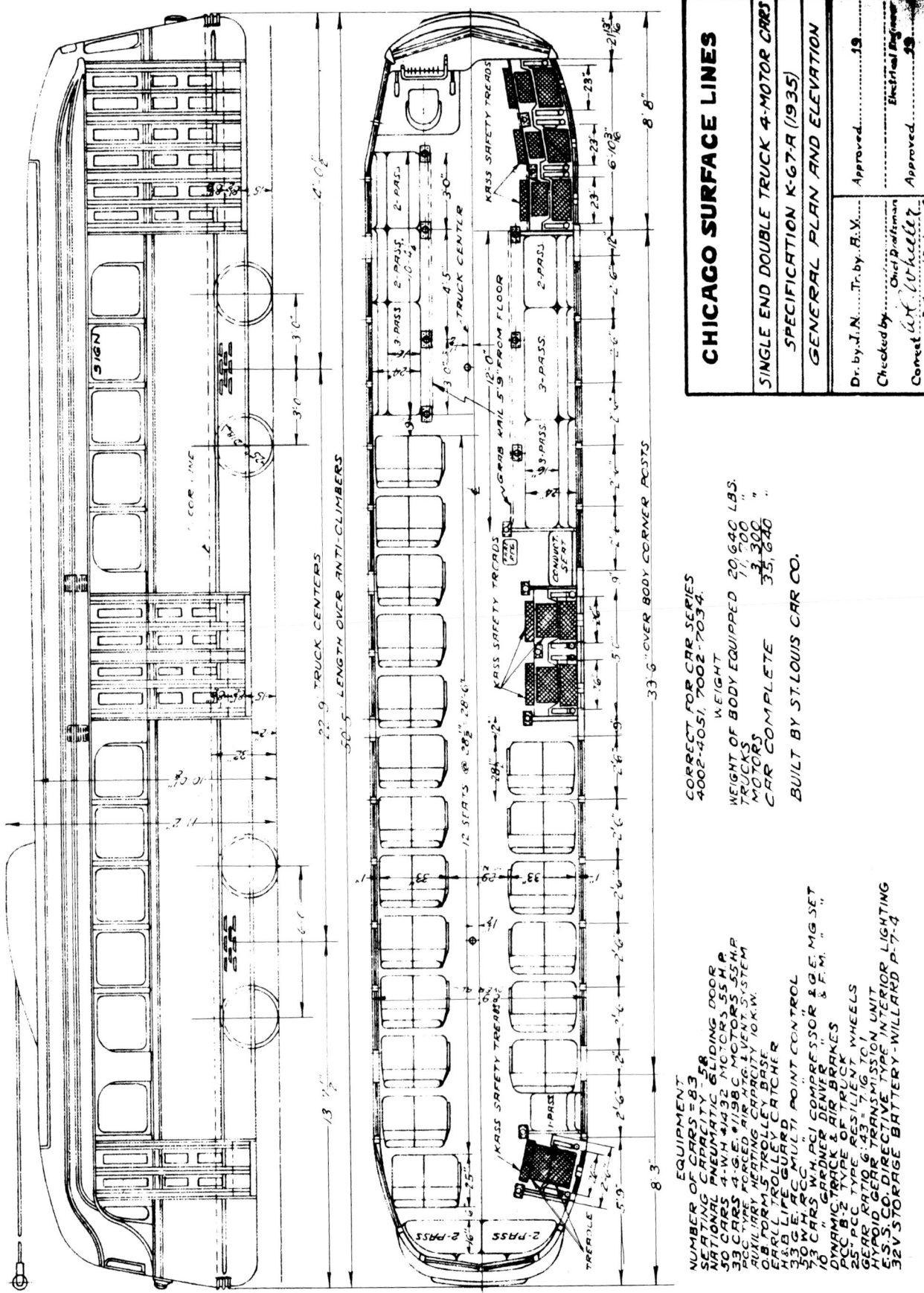

St. Louis Car Company Post-War PCCs

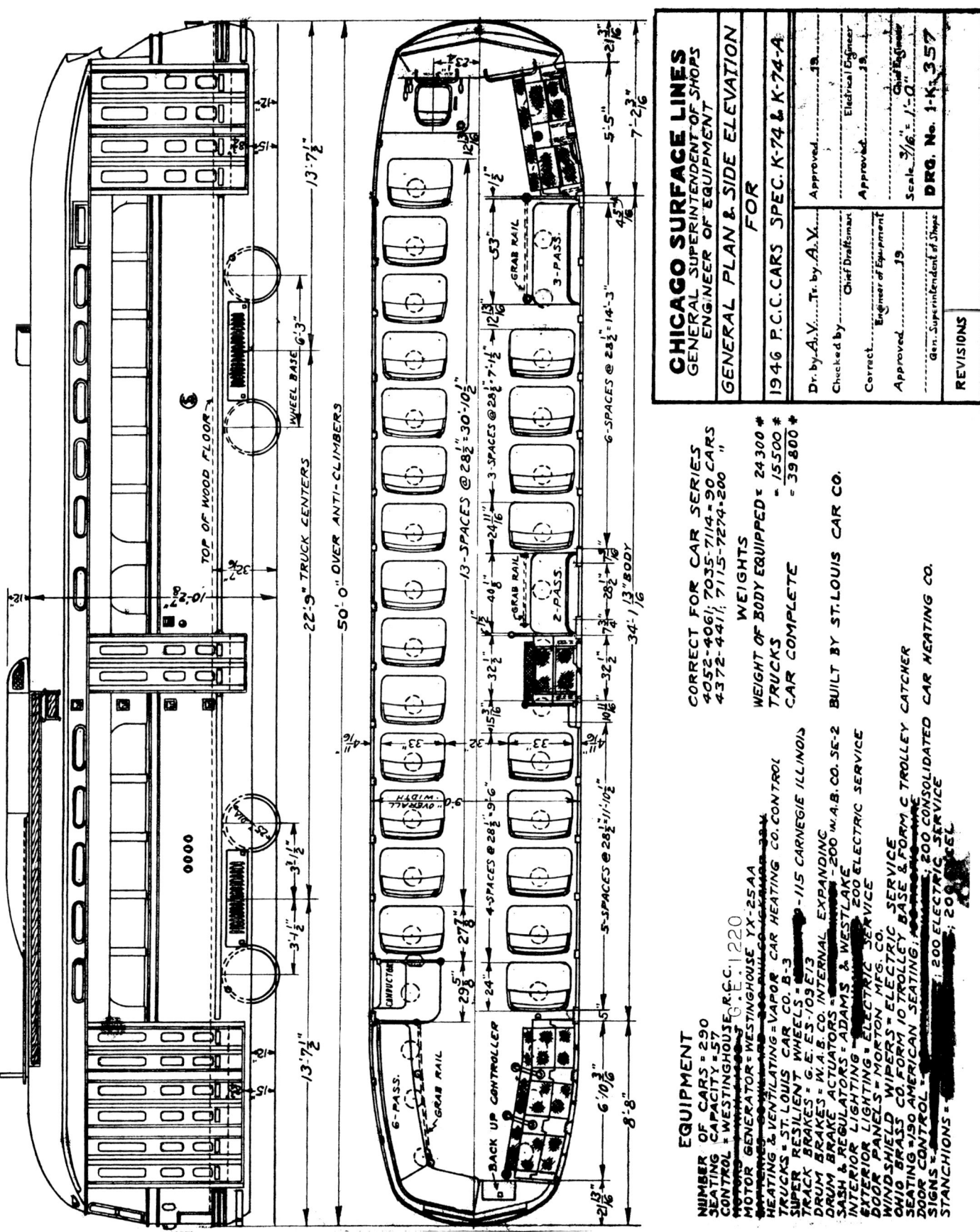

Pullman-Standard Post-War PCCs

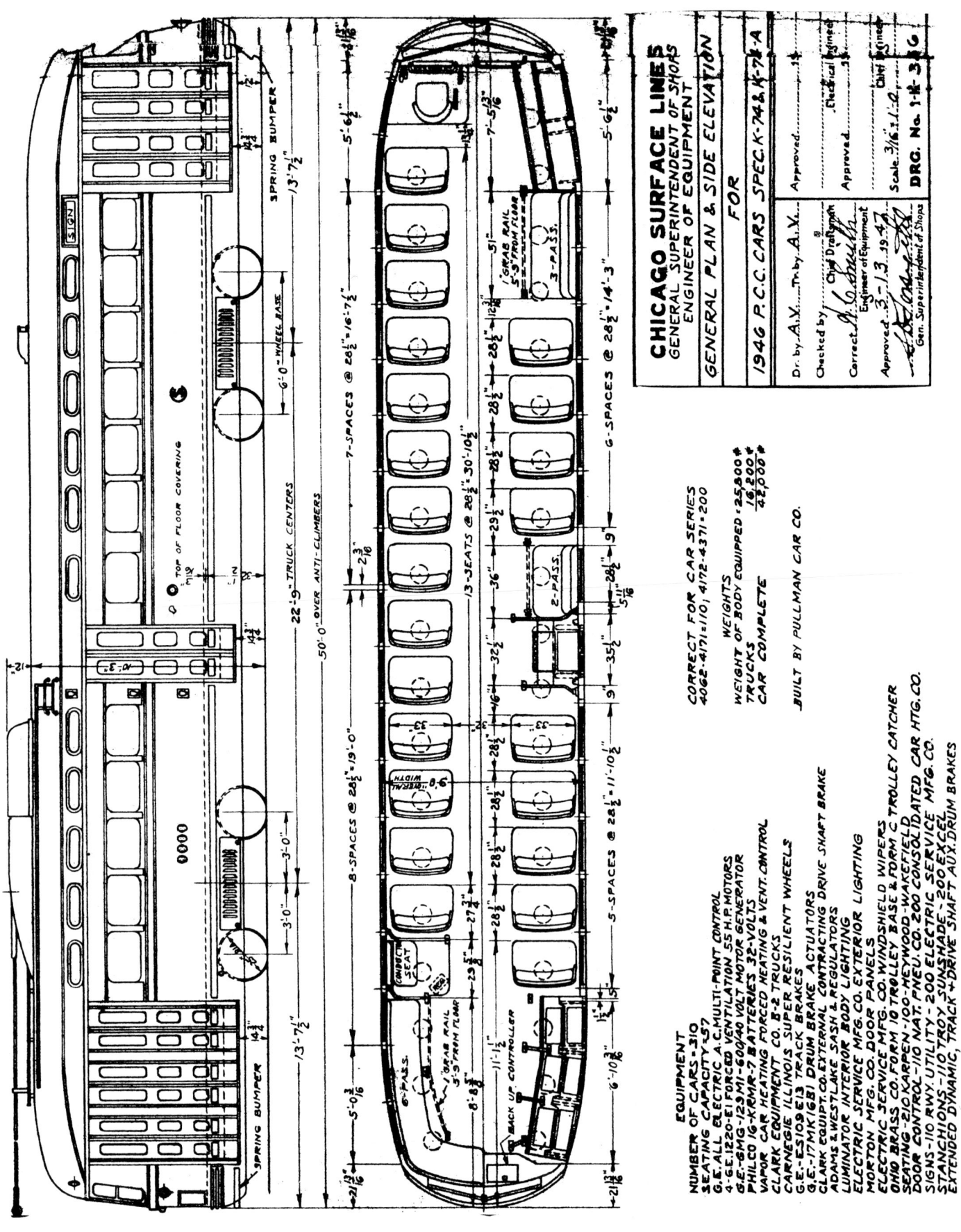

1-man Conversion PCCs

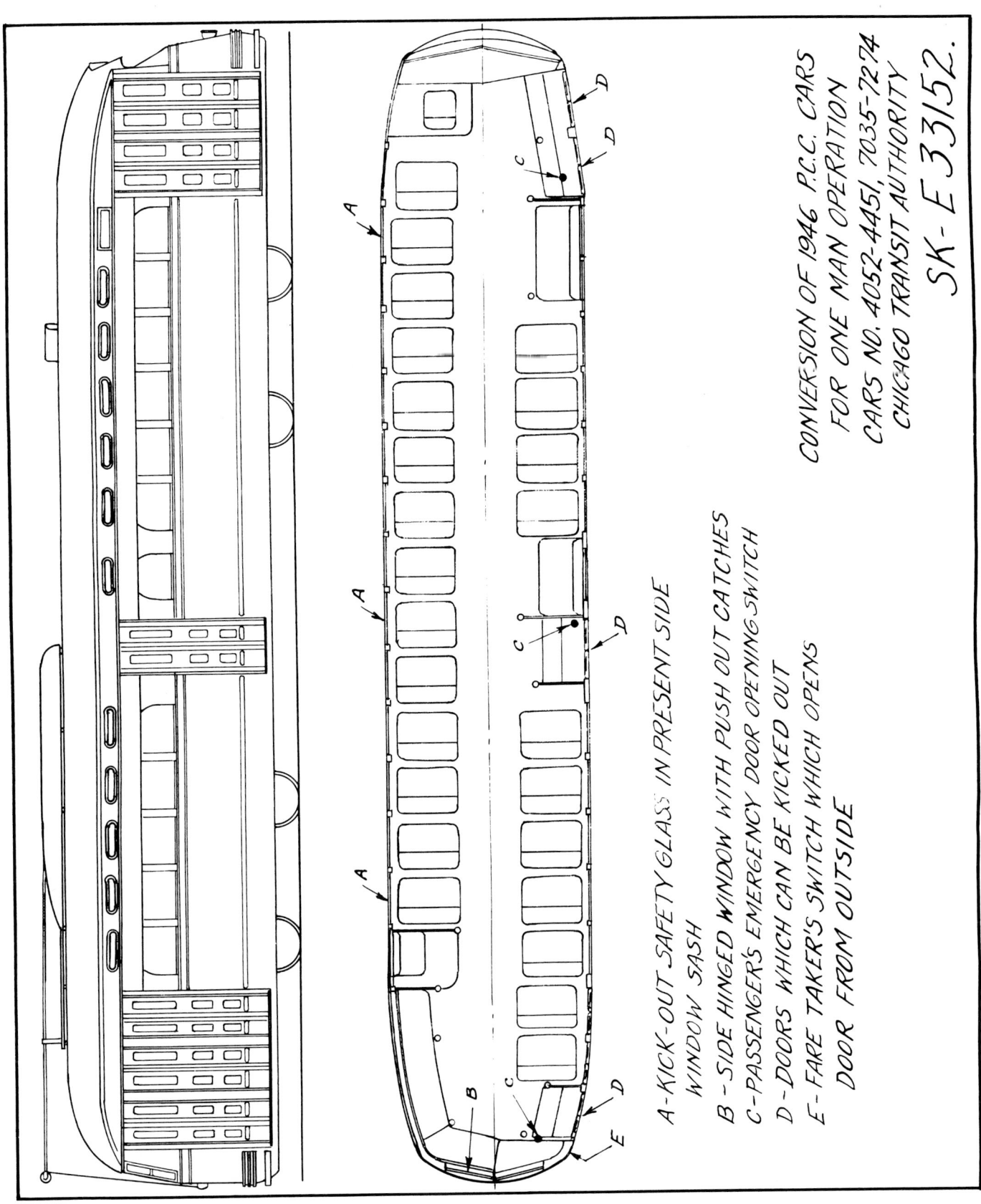

Putting It Together

In October 2013, I was pitched a book by CERA that would be a celebration of the final models of Chicago streetcars: The PCC streetcar. The original pitch was for about 230 pages and a couple hundred photos. I would work as the Photo Editor and graphic artist for the project. I then created a proposal based on the pitch and presented it to the Board for approval with the proviso that I would not be able to begin this project until the video editing project I was doing was completed. It was also understood that I wanted to be completed with this before I left for a long-planned, 2-month trip to New Zealand and Australia in March of 2014.

There is a saying about best laid plans. This book is nothing like the pitch. The book was not completed before my March 2014 trip. This book became much more involved than I thought it would be.

This book came together in stages. The first stage was the selection of the photographic material and the writing of the first chapter. The editors made calls for material and borrowed slides, paper, and photographic prints for me to scan along with plumbing the depths of the Krambles-Peterson Archive. Others submitted scanned materials. With all the material being gathered, some of it obviously had to be rejected. All told the editors selected over a thousand photographs for publication.

With the original page count, it was impossible to include all the material unless it was reproduced in a very small size. With the quality of the material selected, that was an untenable solution. Something had to change. The editors made the decision that we would select the size of the photos first and let the book's page count grow. And grow it did until it became the 448 page book that you hold in your hands.

After the photographic selection, the editors wrote the captions. Some of the photographs had information written on the slide frame or on the back of the prints. Others, however, had no identifying information at all. The editors used their knowledge of when cars were delivered, the style of the automobiles, the color of the automobiles' license plates, and other items in the photo such as the movie playing at a theater to date the photo and provide the best identifying information possible.

Once I had all the information, I started the layout and more importantly the photo retouching. A slide may look good in your hand or projected, but the scanner's eye sees every flaw.

This is a book that would have been almost impossible before the advent of today's electronic tools. The color correction of this many photographs would have cost more than the entire cost of this book run including the printing and shipping costs. That doesn't even take in consideration that we were able to include slides that could not have been corrected without the use of Photoshop. The film stocks utilized included Agfa, Technicolor, Kodachrome, and Ektachrome (pre-dye stabilization).

Then there would have been the expense of the photo retouching. There are very few, if any, photographs included in this book that have not been retouched. A few needed minimal retouching, just a few specks here and there, but many of them required scratch removal as well as heavy cleaning of specks and dirt. A few of them had even been through a fire and had smoke damage that required heavy editing.

The next couple of pages include some before and after shots just to give you an idea of the color and retouching work required to bring this book to you.

All hail the Photoshop!

Bradley Criss, Photo Editor

The top scan from page 434 after the first step of color correction has been completed. This is base file for the retouching, cropping, and final color work before it is completed.

The final version of the slide as it appears on page 358.

The bottom scan from page 434 after the first step of basic color correction and cropping to fit the layout. Until the scan has been retouched for the dirt specks and scratches, a final color correction cannot be done.

The slide has been scanned, cropped, color corrected and retouched. This is how this photo appears earlier in the book.

Bibliography

Chicago Surface Lines, an Illustrated History, Alan R. Lind, Transport History Press, Forest Park, IL, 1974

PCC, The Car that Fought Back, Stephen P. Carlson and Fred W. Schneider III, Interurbans Special 64, Interurban Press, Glendale, CA, 1980

PCC from Coast to Coast, Fred W. Schneider III, Interurbans Special 86, Interurban Press, Glendale, CA, 1983

A Century of Chicago Streetcars, 1858-1958, James D. Johnson, The Traction Orange Company, Wheaton, IL, 1964

Car Plans of the Chicago Surface Lines, Bulletin 38, The Electric Railway Historical Society, Chicago, IL, 1960

Report on the Services, Operations and Policies of the Chicago Transit Authority, DeLeuw Cather and Company Engineers, Chicago, IL, July 1951

Surface Service Magazine, Chicago Surface Lines, Chicago, IL
Vol. 12, Feb 1936, No. 11
Vol. 12, Mar 1936, No. 12
Vol. 13, Oct 1936, No. 7
Vol. 13, Nov 1936, No. 8
Vol. 17, Aug 1940, No. 5
June 1945, August 1945, October-November 1945, December 1945, January 1946, October 1946, November 1946, December 1946, May 1947

Chicago Transit Authority Annual Reports, Chicago Transit Board, Chicago, IL 1947, 1948, 1949, 1950, 1951, 1952, 1953, 1954, 1955, 1956, 1957, 1958

Transit News Nov-Dec 1952, Chicago Transit Authority, , Chicago, IL

Transit News Apr 1953, Chicago Transit Authority, Chicago, IL

Transit News Jul 1953, Chicago Transit Authority, Chicago, IL

Transit News Jul 1958, Chicago Transit Authority, Chicago, IL

PCC Cars of North America, Harold E. Cox, Community Press, Philadelphia, PA, 1963

Chicago's Motor Coaches, Vol. 1: CTA Rolling Stock/1947-1973, Andris J. Kristopans, The Copy Shop, Chicago, IL, 1973

The Green Hornet Streetcar Disaster, Craig Allen Cleve, NIU Press, DeKalb, IL, 2012.

Ride Me at the Illinois Railway Museum, Union, Illinois

Chicago Streetcar Memories DVD

Learn the fascinating history of Chicago's Streetcar System from the horse drawn streetcars in 1859 to the final PCC streetcar in 1958, and share in the memories of eight Chicago Railfans. Featuring interviews with Roy Benedict, Ray DeGroote, Bob Heinlein, Dick Lukin, George Kanary, Ken Spengler, Jeff Wien, and Jim Windmeier, this documentary illustrates the history of the system and personal stories of the railfans with historic footage, artifacts, and photographs from the Electric Railway Historical Society, the Krambles-Peterson Archive, and the Wien-Criss Archive.

Relive the thrills of seeing Red Cars running through the neighborhoods, Blue Geese flying down Madison Street and Green Hornets buzzing down Western Avenue.

Originally presented on the 50th anniversary of the end of Chicago's streetcar system at the June 2008 meeting of the Central Electric Railfans' Association, this Director's Cut contains rewritten and re-recorded narration, additional scenes and footage, including expanded footage shot from and of the last Chicago streetcar.

The documentary runs 130 minutes, not including the DVD extras. Extra features include select footage of Clark-Wentworth and Western Avenue car lines in the 1950s, Chicago Surface Lines' "Safe Highways," a silent public film from the 1920s with an original musical score, roster slide shows with detailed car plans of the major series of streetcars operated by CSL, CTA and their predecessor companies, and footage of the Roosevelt Road "Museum/Soldier Field" loop adjacent to South Lake Shore Drive that was shut down in 1953.

Chapter Index

1. Prologue
2. In 1859...
3. The Railfans
4. The Streetcar Tunnels
5. Unification
6. Routes, Runs and Motormen
7. Introducing the PCC
8. Chicago's 1936 PCCs
9. Other PCC Operations in North America
10. Post-War PCCs
11. Memorable Stories
12. May 25, 1950
13. The Beginning of the End
14. The Old Reds
15. The McCarter Plan
16. The Final Run
17. Thoughts and Reflections